Best Wishes
Rose

Sono Pizzitano

(Man of Pizzo)

by

Michael Power

+ thanks for all
your encouragement
Michael Power

Sono Pizzitano

(Man of Pizzo)

by

Michael Power

First Published in 2009 by TAF Publishing

ISBN: 978-0-9562303-4-8
A CIP Catalogue record for this book is available from the British Library

Published with the assistance of The Author's Friend.
For more information about assisted publishing, including catalogue and titles, visit www.TheAuthorsFriend.com

Typesetting and Cover Design by Oscar Duggan

Printed and bound in Ireland by Gemini International Ltd

Sono Pizzitano (Man of Pizzo)

TABLE OF CONTENTS

Foreword and Dedication

Why Italy............. and Pizzo, in particular?

Italy seduced me years ago. I had some Italian students who impressed me greatly. They were very friendly, good humoured, fun-loving, confident, young people who seemed to have a very good attitude and yet were quite relaxed. When my wife and I started going on sun holidays we were thrilled with the real heat which rose up to us from the airport apron the moment we got off the plane. The hotel on the Tunisian beach in 40 degree temperatures was paradise after the wet, cold summer in an Irish caravan, much like the one featured in a certain episode of “Craggy Island”. Never again would we settle for less than real heat for our holidays. Italy has this to offer but also much more.

When we first went some years ago it was in the middle of August, the traditional Italian holiday time. We discovered Vernazza, one of five seaside villages called “Le Cinque Terre”, which had me thinking I was walking into a film set the first time I turned into its narrow street of 4 storey houses almost touching each other across the way. We swam, sunbathed, ate and drank well, snacked on ice creams and enjoyed the simple pleasures of life in the sun by the sea in a beautiful little village with happy Italians at home or on holiday. We relaxed completely and every evening we ate out by the harbour with music and fine food in a ceremony of dining and taste such as we had never experienced before.

Old historic villages and towns of character, noble buildings, and wonderful piazzas abound in Italy and enhance the natural beauties of the sunny climate, the clear blue sea, miles of sandy beaches, the mountains in the background, dotted with red-roofed villages perched impossibly on steep inclines, making one wonder and yearn to explore their secrets. The food is the finest and lovingly prepared. We have visited many other areas but came to Calabria in 2007, travelling south from Naples and leaving the tourist trap of

Sorrento for places more unexplored by English speakers.

On holiday in Tropea, with its beautiful beaches, and historic centre, another favourite destination for Italians, we heard about a town, built like Tropea, on a rise above the sea and the beach. On being driven into, it by an agent we had contacted about property, we were thrilled. It was love at first sight. The sea is so inviting and blue and an ancient castle, set amid old houses in the centro storico rises majestically up from the marina. A little harbour with a sandy beach (one of many dotted along the curving coastline) at the foot of dramatic high cliffs of tufo, topped by the old tall buildings of the centro storico made me want to stop and stare. A deep impression was made and I still love to stand and admire the picture-postcard setting. The sun shines all summer and well into winter. The sea is blue and clear. Waves are dancing sometimes and sprinkled diamonds sparkle here and there when it is calm.

The piazza buzzes with life, an attractive amphitheatre of easy living and relaxed locals and tourists. The food is cheap and cheerful when eating out. Fresh fish, fruit and vegetables are easily found. Festivals and music nights abound and entertain in Summer. Bars, ice-cream parlours, restaurants and shops vie for browsing customers, but not in a aggressive or impolite manner as in some holiday resorts, and chairs and sunny umbrellas spread out enticingly.

Nothing happens and everything is going on at the same time. But it is the people who make it a paradise. Friendliness is in the air and welcomes are everywhere. “Buon Giorno”, “Buona Sera”, “Salve” and “Salute” are on everyone’s lips. “Ciao” calls out. Church bells ring, lovers stroll arm in arm, couples kiss, drivers have rows yet depart smiling. Older men sit, smoke, gesticulate, shout, talk, stare and sort the world out. Many are ex-sailors or have been emigrants, have seen the world, and are glad to be back where they belong. Strikingly-beautiful young ladies, slim as models, sally forth, poised to perfection. Confident young studs preen and strut while children run and cycle around, "having a ball" into the small hours.

It is not like some new holiday resort with apartment blocks and no previous or existing life to which one can belong. This town has a life and community to offer, a past and present, a people who welcome strangers, and most definitely, a future. My wife and I came here on visits, returning in 2008 to buy a house and have a long summer holiday. In no time we have made friends and feel accepted, having been almost adopted by one particularly helpful couple, who introduced themselves to us at one of the football matches we viewed in the piazza. We are almost afraid to tell too many people in case they all come and change Pizzo by outnumbering its own lovely people. We want to preserve for ourselves and for Pizzititani what we have found and fallen in love with. It is a great escape from wet, Irish/British summers and dull, grey cities. It is a place I can completely relax in.

In launching this book I would like to thank all who have helped me along the way, especially my family and friends in Dublin and in Pizzo. Particular thanks are due to Breda, my sister, who always encouraged me to write over the years and to Paul, now of Calabrian Services, who urged me to get this book published and gave me practical help. Several others were very interested and supportive of me in my travels, and in my efforts to get an Italian property and to tell my story by publishing this book.

Organisations I have been involved with, who have been a part of my life generally and have helped, particularly, in my writing efforts.

Dunboyne Tennis Club, Clonee (also Castleknock. TC).
Blanchardstown Library
Springlawn Residents Association and my good neighbours
Dublin 15 Community Council
Blanchardstown Area Partnership
St Malachy's NS, Finglas South
The writers' groups in Blanchardstown and Cabra Library
The Adult Education Centre, Main St., Blanchardstown.
St.Vincent de Paul,Navan Road
The Irish Times, especially the letters page
All my former students and teaching colleagues and the INTO.
.

Finally, I dedicate this book, in particular, to the good citizens of Pizzo who welcomed me and my family to their town and who make it such a happy place to be. I also include the Irish, English, Germans and other hangers-on, ex-pats, exiles and all who have been lucky enough to find this wonderful spot… as my sister Breda says "All this and heaven too!"

Ps: for reasons of privacy and to protect the innocent many names have been changed in this book

Cast Of Characters

(many names have been changed to protect the innocents' privacy)

Alessia	Maria's and Euroinvest secretary
Alessio	a geometra and husband of Maria
Anna	my youngest daughter
Anna Marie	Bernard's daughter
Bernard	my second son
Dermot	our first son
Donna	my wife
Felix	B&B owner
Frances	My elder daughter .. our fourth child. Now in Australia
Frank Mc Court "Teacher	The author of"Angela's Ashes" "Teacher Man" etc
Franco, Carmen, Loredana	Staff of the Pantheon Bar
Francesco, Franco etc	too many of them in Pizzo
Liam	now Anna's husband
Lily	Dermot's daughter
Maria	the agent who introduced us to house and arranged sale and works etc
Mark	my third son
Mr (Paola) Plant	architect/vendor/works manager
Nicola	Dermot's partner
Olive	Partner of Bernard
Paddy Agnew	Irish Times journalist and author
Paul, Lorraine, Leon, Beata	of Calabrian Invest: a very helpful agency and all good friends
Sandro	my Italian friend
Sara	wife of Sandro
"Sono Pizzitano"	myself .. the author of this book
Toni	a local property owner in Pizzo

CHAPTER 1
Finding Pizzo

"The sun is warm, the sky is clear,
The waves are dancing fast and bright
Blue isles and snowy mountains wear
The purple noon's transparent might"
(from "Stanzas Written in Dejection near Naples"
by P. B. Shelley)

Summer 2007 was terrible in Ireland. Cold, grey and cloudy skies were the order of the day and it rained a lot through June, July and August. May had been as beautiful as it can be in Ireland, which is great when we get it, but it does not happen often enough. Bright, warm, sunny days followed each other for about two or more weeks. With our usual pessimism and knowledge of the Irish weather, many of us knew our summer might already be over. Even though my daughter upbraided me for saying so, I said it and that is how it turned out.

My wife's mother had died slowly during those glorious days in May when we, her daughters, son, sons-in-law and daughter-in-law and her own sister and others, had all had a chance to see her and each other and talk, remember and grieve. It had been a tough time for all, but the weather and the fact we had a chance to say "Good bye" and get together once more, probably for the last time in such numbers, had made a difference, and now it was over, and my wife and I were on our way to Italy, which had been our favourite destination for many years.

We had booked a hotel in Sorrento for 2 days at the beginning of June, flying into Naples, which was a new experience for us. Mostly we had been in central and Northern Italy before, which we had enjoyed greatly, but now we had decided to try somewhere different.

Our Sorrento hotel was not so great and it was not exactly convenient to the town, but supposedly it had its own beach, which turned out to be not so great an attraction as it was very small and the sand almost black. In fact, I read an article recently which claimed there were no beaches in Naples and I wouldn't really disagree. We also had to endure a thunder and lightening storm which was quite dramatic but not what we wanted on our holidays. After two days there, wandering around as tourists, surrounded by other tourists and paying crazy tourist prices I decided it had to get out.

I went on the internet and checked out places in Calabria which I had previously investigated, months and weeks earlier at home. I phoned one apartment owner in Tropea, whose apartment, and especially, a blue sea and the clean, long, sandy beach I had viewed on his website, I had been greatly taken by. He seemed friendly and agreed to meet us at the train station which probably sealed the deal. We made our way back into Naples and then eventually booked tickets to Tropea, a resort well-known to Italians, many of whom come there every year from the north of Italy for their holidays. I say "eventually" as we had some difficulty buying the tickets. A none-too-friendly official in the ticket office refused to help my wife as she tried to get information, sticking his nose in the air and waving her away with his hand to his throat and refusing to have anything to do with her (maybe because she was at the wrong window, but we were finding our way in a foreign land and trying out our less-than-perfect Italian). I find most Italians helpful but there are such people everywhere.

After a pleasant enough train journey, despite it being crowded, we arrived in Tropea about 4 hours later and our friendly apartment owner was at hand to collect us. He drove us to our destination, through a delightful, typically Italian town, with its narrow alleys, piazzas and historic buildings, especially in the "centro storico" (historic centre). He informed us about the huge increase in population it enjoyed every summer. His apartments to let were actually in an old palazzo, which delighted us. He explained how he had bought the building as an investment and part-time home, where he himself was living, but not his wife and children at that time. He made us feel very welcome. He gave us the local information about the beach and the general area in good English and a discount card for some restaurants in the area, which we got great use of.

The apartment was not too big, but sufficient for our needs, with a mezzanine floor used as a sleeping area. It was a little dark, which we found irksome after a while, but the open air entrance into the old palazzo, behind the massive door, was brighter at times and he allowed us make use of it for sitting in and reading and we also dried our clothes there, but later he objected to this. He had a computer with an internet connection installed afterwards which pleased me greatly, but even before that he would allow me use his own when he was around.

We were delighted with our new-found accommodation and soon set out to explore the town. There were many steps down to the beaches so we did not venture there on our first night but wandered around the town, enjoying the great views of the sea and surrounding countryside from various high vantage points, and trying out our discount card in the nearest restaurant and being thrilled with the food and the price. We had our drinks in another, where I made friends with the owner, Franco, introducing myself as "Michelle" as I wanted him and others to know we had some Italian and we wanted to show respect for the country, its people and language. We often sat and drank there over the next two weeks or so, while relaxing, people-watching and viewing the goings-on in the square.

The next day we made for the beach. There were many steps down from the "centro storico" and my knees were not the best but the beach was beautiful and it was well worth the struggle down the steps. Pure, clean, blue, almost still Mediterranean waters beckoned. The sand was of the finest golden grains and hot, but not so hot I couldn't walk on it. A few people were scattered around, as it was early in the season, and across the road there was a café with cold beer just waiting for my custom. At the far end of the beach a huge rocky outcrop rose from up from the sea and the beach, with an old building at its top and a long winding path of steps up to it. It made for a great dramatic scene. Later we discovered it was a convent, which gave rise to stories and imaginings on my part and a wish that my sister, Breda, a nun, would see it and even join the community (if there was one left) so we could get in!

At the other end of the beach was a private area with chalets and a bar and other facilities and, on further a marina or harbour, with the mountains rising behind. We were well pleased with our choice of venue for our holiday. The sun shone down all day and we stayed for hours, me swimming at times, and both of us sun-bathing and relaxing with a beer or snack now and then. There was a little dip just as one entered the cool blue water so almost immediately one found a good depth and little waves added to the pure, physical pleasure of diving in, especially after coming from Ireland with its cold, cloudy, grey skies. I found a bit of pumice stone one day, which brought thoughts of the Romantic Poets to my mind and a certain poem I had learnt for my Leaving Certificate Examination in Ireland many years before. I felt I was joining them in a way, on their grand tours! I still have the pumice stone.

My wife, Donna, besides being beautiful, has a sallow complexion, which absorbs the sun so well, and she enjoys the whole sunny, seaside experience and relaxes completely. It is her perfect holiday activity and I felt I had done well in finding it for her. We were in heaven and we knew it. Later on, we walked on and found other delightful beaches, some private and commercial and with more beach facilities, such as bars, shops, umbrellas and deck chairs, water sports equipment, canoes, and all the usual paraphernalia associated with same, as well as hawkers of towels and jewellery, drinks and anything else that would sell. Everybody was pleasant and there was plenty of room if one wished to get away from it all. The island of Stromboli was in the distance and boats plied their way back and forth, which only impressed us more and made for a maritime idyll.

We really enjoyed ourselves in Tropea, wandering down to the beach every day, mostly frequenting ones which had a beachside café with snacks and beer or wine. At night we had our meals in a different restaurant each time, but usually ones which gave us a discount with our card. The meals were invariably great. We discovered "alici" (sardines) as a starter, "fagioli" (beans) and many more dishes and had "risotto alla pescatore" many times, as we had been introduced to it before in Italy, and were delighted with the food, the smiling service and the prices. As a child and a young man, I had not been very adventurous about trying new foods but, since coming to Italy, especially to "Le Cinque Terra", I had improved a lot and amazed myself, with the result that I was now much more open to doing so. Now I can eat all kinds of pasta and other Italian dishes every day and night and not feel the need for traditional Irish food. Afterwards, we walked around the town, shopping or just gazing and usually ending up with a drink at Franco's "Café de Paris", where we got to know Franco and most of the staff who were very attentive to our needs. It was there we often had breakfast too, just standing up having a cappuccino and croissant at the bar.

After a few days, we began to look at estate agents' windows and dreamed of living in Tropea. We had always intended looking in this area or Puglia, as we had heard it was cheaper than other areas and it was one of the reasons we had come there. We called in to some agents and went to view some properties. We discussed it with the owner of our apartment who gave us advice willingly and explained why so few properties were on sale in Tropea. Because it is a very successful Italian resort and owners get good rents, they are not really interested in selling, especially in the centro storico.

One or two properties did interest us and a nice local agent showed us an old mill in the town. It did not grab my attention but my wife was quite interested. Another property we viewed was outside Tropea, too far out for us, we decided.

Then we discovered a new office advertising "new-build" apartments, near the beach, but outside the centro storico. We went to visit the site which was still in construction and were quite well pleased. We researched the orientation and settled on some apartments we might be interested in, the ones with a south-west aspect, to get the rays of the evening sun. The cheapest ones were smaller ones at the back of the development with little chance of the sun shining in. It seemed a nice development but the ones we wanted were either too dear or taken already because they had a great view of the sea. We even got friendly with the secretary in the "Immobiliare" (agency), Cettina, when she showed us around and we discussed how I might do English lessons there and she wanted to work with me as my secretary/Italian point of contact. The man in the internet shop where we went sometimes was also interested in the apartments and told us about it. He wanted one in the shade, like most Italians, whereas, we "crazy" foreigners wanted the sun shining in, but we were glad to hear a local was interested and thought them a good investment. We also went to other developments, mostly within 20 kilometres of Tropea, including green-field sites which would one day contain a "touristico villagio" and, while they seemed fine and had tennis courts and other facilities, we decided we wanted to live with Italians, preferably in the centro storico, and where people would be living all-year round and not just in summer or among tourists. We continued searching and enjoying our holiday. Anyway, after a few days I get tired of doing nothing and sun-bathing and having something to do makes life more interesting for me.

Another couple took an apartment near us in our palazzo and we got talking to them. They were also interested in acquiring an Italian property and had done some searching themselves, as had many week-end trippers we saw around the town, who were on viewing expeditions from England mostly, and usually going around with bronzed young representatives of the agency developing the new-builds we had viewed. We were glad not to have to endure that hard selling and being accompanied by somebody pushing us into buying. Many times in bars and cafes we found ourselves listening to strained conversations, as clients were being pressured into making deals and having to listen to all sorts of promises.

One day, in conversation with this new couple who were renting an apartment beside us, they mentioned a visit to Pizzo might be worth our while. They said it was much like Tropea with a centro storico, high above wonderful beaches and a marina. It seemed interesting and I decided to investigate it on the internet. I came across some properties for sale with an agent and emailed the agent. Maria was her name. She arranged to call to Tropea and collect us in order to show us some of the properties she had. She was as good as her word and duly arrived with her handsome Italian husband, Alessio, who drove us to Pizzo. It was a pleasant drive and both spoke English which helped. She was English, of Italian parents and was very helpful and friendly. The town of Pizzo entranced us, right from the first moment we laid our eyes on it, with its beaches, marina and the castle rising up from the cliffs above the shore and up to the historic centre and piazza. We fell in love with it straight away and felt we were well on our way to achieving our Italian dream.

CHAPTER 2
Our Background And Interest In Italy

My wife and I had been to Italy many times by 2008 and the idea of buying there had been mooted and discussed. There had been false starts and mishaps, rows and thrills, but we had become enchanted with it and kept dreaming. Once, I had even announced to my fellow teachers that I would not be returning in September as I hoped to move to Italy to teach English. That had not worked out quite as well as I thought. But let me go back further and explain a little about us and our life together.

We were married in 1973. I was a primary school teacher and Donna was a secretary in a building firm at the time. We did manage to buy a house after a spell living in a flat in Rathgar (next door to where Jack Lynch, a former Taoiseach, or Prime Minister of Ireland, lived). Donna gave up work to stay at home and have and mind our children so we had to manage on one salary, as was quite normal at the time, but an arrangement which has become less common in the profession since. Our family amounted to five children, Dermot, Bernard, Mark, Frances and Anna, after 12 years, during which we were just getting by mostly. Money was scarce and continued to be, right into the nineties. With all our children starting school and some quite grown up, Donna went back to work, which made a difference to our standard of living but it was not until the year 2000 we managed to go on our first sun holiday. Before that it had been a week in Galway during race week when I would be working at my part-time job on the Tote (a semi-state company involved in betting on horse racing), or down to Waterford, where I had some connections as my family had originally come from there. They were alright as holidays for us, but nothing like our first sun holiday away, just us two, in Tunisia! The moment we got off that plane and felt the heat from the airport apron we were smitten and holidays would never be the same.

I had been abroad before as a young teacher but had headed to

northern European countries mostly, as I hitch-hiked, and it would have taken me too long to get south to Biarritz or anywhere on the Mediterranean, much as I wanted to, and anyway money was too scarce then, in the absence of Ryanair especially, to fly there. I had been to Paris and its hinterland, Versailles, Chartres and on another holiday I had hitched up to Amsterdam, stopping off in Calais, Brussels, Ostend, and Utrecht, having been in London with some flat mates and taken the hovercraft from Dover. I had enjoyed all those trips, but on my own and yes, there had been adventures, such as when I lost my travellers cheques or had them stolen. I did manage to stay in Amsterdam for a few weeks extra by working for lodgings in the youth hostel. When I asked for work there, they asked me how many languages I spoke.
"Two, English and Irish" I replied, and the Dutch, those linguists of Europe fell around the place laughing.
"Don't think you will be working on reception then!" they spluttered.
That stayed with me for some time so that now I try to learn some of the language of the country to which I go. I worked in the dormitories and helped at breakfast time and got food and lodgings for my trouble and was very happy with that arrangement. There was a further embarrassment to come when my school principal's daughters turned up at the hostel and we got to know each other. It was fine really until I went back to school in September and he got this hippy teacher with a new beard and long hair who had met his daughters on holiday. It didn't cause a huge problem though, not for me anyway.

Donna was not a traveller when we met and hadn't been much outside Dublin apart from a holiday in Birmingham, where she enjoyed herself with her cousin Angela, also over from Dublin, both of them staying with their Aunt Bridie. Angela was talkative and Donna was the quite one, at least that's the way she tells it. They were free! Two young girls at the time, just learning to flirt and flaunt their power over the poor (or lucky) young fellows they met at the ice rink or elsewhere. It was a brief glimpse of freedom.

Donna's father had died when she was ten, just as mine had, when I was about the same age. She had to leave school at an early age or chose to, but went to night school, and she was working as a secretary in a builder's company when I met her. Life was tough enough, as her mother also worked to bring in the money and Donna, the eldest, got a whole load of extra responsibilities, becoming almost a second parent. She cleaned and cooked and was a good, serious girl (Now she may be breaking out!). I had had relatives in Waterford to whom I was sent for holidays and loved it mostly. She had hardly moved outside Dublin and is still wary of country living, although we did live in County Meath for almost 17 years. Now she tells me she still has nightmares about that house and still does sometimes but at the time it seemed fine and I didn't know it got to her sometimes. (There is much more to this but that may be for another book)

Having enjoyed Tunisia we decided to go back before Christmas that year with our two daughters. It was different! It was not as hot amazingly, we found, to our surprise. Even the hotel could not compare with the one we had been in, in summer. In fact, Donna wanted to go home when she saw our room and cried for quite some time. The home bird in her got a shock and it took some time for her to recover. She did enquire about going home and was told it would be possible…. for about €2000! The hotel was not up to the standard of the other one and neither were the guests who mostly consisted of English pensioners getting away from winter in Britain. We all settled down after a while and made the best of it. The beach was hardly visited and the pool rarely used, except for some mad Irish who jumped into much colder water than they expected. The girls still managed to enjoy themselves, I think, but we were quite glad to get home. We did visit a market or two, the Medina and the girls got the treatment, being young, white, beautiful and glamorous, and we had to make a break for it before they were entirely overcome with unwelcome attentions. Like mother, like daughters……..but this was not Birmingham!

That was not the first occasion Donna had wanted to leave a hotel and go home straight away. Once we booked a hotel in Virginia, County Cavan, in Ireland. When we got there, Donna took one look around the bedroom and demanded to be taken home. I agreed reluctantly and back we came. We had dropped our sons with her mother for the weekend and now decided not to collect them, say nothing to anybody and we just spent the weekend enjoying ourselves at home and by going to the Phoenix Park races! Oh we were bad! The granny was great and her sisters, the aunts, were too. We were lucky to be always able to get out with a regular supply of doting aunts, who often remind me of this and suggest payback. We rather figured it was payback for the time Donna had to parent them and take on much of the responsibility for the house and family. They may not quite see it like that. We did some babysitting for them with their children but not often, I'm afraid I have to admit. C'est la vie!

I had been teaching for about 40 years at this stage and Donna had cared for our children and brought them up well, making them independent, capable young people who can clean, wash clothes, cook and look after themselves and who are sociable, bright, responsible, intelligent, caring people with good jobs or prospects. Now we feel this is our time again. We have come out the other end of the tunnel. Our children have left home; some have children now themselves, and all are doing well in their careers and lives, as far as we are concerned. We are very proud of them and now we need to get on with our lives and enjoy the next age, whether retired or not.

Donna certainly deserves it as I didn't give her much chance to enjoy single life, snapping her up on her second visit to Sloopy's discotheque in 1972 and marrying her less than a year later and "No", we didn't "have to" as some of her neighbours and others thought. I realise now she went from one set of responsibilities and family to another but she made the choice and I was very happy to oblige and make children! Now she is discovering herself again and having time for herself (maybe for the first time really………. but not neglecting me, I hope!). Oh selfish man!

In recent years we have been to many sunspots such as Majorca, Greece, Turkey, Cyprus, and other parts of Italy. In Italy we first went to Bologna and then Florence, to a campsite suggested to me by one of my Italian students, who arranged to meet me there. But it didn't happen. Donna was not entranced with that or the place, or my failure to book good accommodation, or even any accommodation after the first 2 nights! We had some rows but eventually I found an apartment in Vernazza for us, in Le Cinque Terre, a beautiful area of 5 coastal villages above La Spezia, a place which had been suggested to us by a good friend Chris in Castleknock Tennis Club, of which we were members. It was holiday time in Italy around the 15th of August and I only got the apartment booked after about 50 phone calls! The next problem was to get there and my wife and youngest daughter, Anna, were not too sure about taking more trains so I decided to hire a car in Florence to get to Vernazza. I had not driven in Italy before and it was all a bit nerve-wrecking for us all but we got there. Unfortunately, to get into Vernazza one has to drive up and down mountains, with hairpin bends and small roads with the other cars almost pushing you off the edge, so there were some scares and frightened, animated conversations, almost divorce proceedings, but we got there. Well, almost there, because the village is so small cars are not allowed in and must be parked about 1 or 2 kilometres away. We did that and walked in dragging our suitcases and worn-out bodies and stressed-out minds with us. But what a sight greeted us, a little Italian harbour town with high houses on each side of the main street on the way to the harbour, apartments piled high over shops and restaurants and all filled with the noisy Italian locals and visitors. We had struck gold. It was like a film set. I found the Blue Marlin bar where we had arranged to get our key and was directed across the narrow street to a second floor apartment with 2 bedrooms overlooking the whole film set. Our kindly landlord was fine and the bar man who had directed us, Massimo, was a big, handsome, friendly Italian who kept my wife in raptures for the week. I liked him too and it helped.

We had a fantastic week and often promise ourselves to go back but there are so many more places to see. There was very little really in it but the food was fantastic. Every night tables were set out in the tiny harbour and we ate like royalty, trying food I would never have tried at home and making the effort to take our time like Italians (I wasn't very good at that and was already looking for the next course far too early). That was where I first ate seafood and have never looked back. The seafood risotto we got there has never been equalled, I feel. My daughter and I swam in the harbour. Donna did some serious sun-bathing in the almost unbearable heat of August in Italy. We made boat and train trips to the other villages and into La Spezia. We will never forget Vernazza.

The car? We completely ignored it for the week, having spent a small fortune on it, but found the train was so much easier for getting around. I wish we had known that, that morning in Florence but one lives and learns. We did use it to get back to the airport in Bologna and get home. One unfortunate result of using the car is that my wife prefers me not to hire a car in Italy. I did do it once more in Garda to take my daughter's boyfriend to the airport in Treviso because it would have been impossible to get there on time early enough in the morning. It was an adventure too as we arrived at the wrong airport, the one in Venice used by Aer Lingus, but we made it in plenty of time to Treviso, despite that and a few other scrapes, like entering one way streets the wrong way to get onto the autostrada! We travel by train now but one day she will come around.........I hope!

"He always gets there in the end" as Anna said about me, consoling her mother. Donna's mother, like most mothers, did not encourage her to take risks so I have brought something to this marriage, I think. We may have had our differences but we complement each other too. Role reversal is quite important and I can be very cautious too. Now let us discover more, take more risks, like living and buying in Italy………I pray.

Sardinia was a different kind of holiday. Having worn Donna out with my lack of proper organisation I told her she must select the next holiday, a package one, if she wished. Sometimes she says she just wants a good hotel, a week sunbathing on a nice beach, fine food and drink and nice clothes to wear……….. and maybe someone else, besides me, doing the organising! Not much to ask for really and she got it. She picked Sardinia and the hotel or self-catering in a hotel so we could eat wherever we wanted and we did. There was fine beach across the road from the hotel and a lovely old town centre and marina to go to at night or anytime for shopping, for Italian shoes and stuff like that. The sun shone beautifully and we went to the public beach everyday, seeing the locals enjoying their own facilities, like a little bar which provided snacks and cool drinks at reasonable rates. The marina and old town were gorgeous and had plenty of bars for me to stop in and refresh myself, while waiting for Donna as she shopped. The meals in the fine restaurants along the quays were great as well as the views. The supermarkets even excelled with their selection of food, hot and cold and a new element to us, a little bar just inside the door (the crèche for the men?). To be fair, Donna enjoyed it too. The Finals of the European Nations Championship in soccer was on at the time (2004) and we enjoyed that too. Donna doesn't mind watching 22 young men in shorts running around after a ball, as most of them are handsome and athletic enough. I am a football fan. We watched the final over dinner in the hotel and Greece winning might give Ireland some hope we can do likewise, as Mr Trappatoni (the new Irish soccer manager) remarked, I believe.

One day out walking in the old town, Donna got a bit weak and had to sit down. A kind lady asked was she alright and we were glad to say she was. Imagine our surprise when we walked into an estate agent's around the corner and there the lady was. She was being very helpful and Donna had seen a property she was interested in.

We got all the information and my wife was very interested to learn it only cost €20,000. I was less enthusiastic as it was up the mountains and very isolated and probably required some work. That was the start of our searching for foreign property! I often remind her of it and make fun of her choice, especially in light of her nightmares about living in the country in Ireland but she says still it would have been a bargain! I did get interested in a school for English which was looking for a new owner on the island and followed it up on the internet afterwards but to no avail. Sardinia is a great holiday destination, especially now with direct flights by Ryanair from Ireland, and Alghero was great for us.

I got bolder and announced to my work colleagues I wasn't coming back in September as I was going to teach in Italy! Donna agreed she would try it for 3 weeks and see what she thought. We picked Pescara this time for some reason I cannot completely remember now. I think it had something to do with cheap living and that Italian student we didn't meet in Florence previously. We were to go to his uncle's property in a town near there on the coast, but when that fell through we just went to Pescara anyway. The town was fine enough and we got a hotel for 2 nights (my old plan) and then had to look around for accommodation for a longer period, an apartment. We were not very successful and, having traipsed Pescara, we eventually found an agent who helped us find an apartment in Silvi, a seaside resort about 10 kilometres outside Pescara. This agent was very helpful and told me he would get me a job in the local university, teaching English. He loved Dublin, told his staff stories of the mad-drinking Irish, and probably thought me a great guy just because I was from there. The apartment was alright but the resort was deserted as the season was over in September with children gone back to school. When it rained for a few days that put the cap on it and Donna decided she had had enough. We decided to cut our losses and come home. The weather cleared up then, of course, but we had booked our tickets and flew home. I even have a great picture of Donna on the deserted sunny beach which will always haunt me, as I think, if we had just stuck it out a bit longer it might have worked out. I'm sure I would have got teaching, and maybe even in a university, but that's life. The last day before flying home we went into Pescara and Donna came to appreciate it and could have stayed there but we didn't. We found nice restaurants, a lovely populated city beach and interesting shops, but it was not to be. Maybe it was all for the better. I didn't go back to work until after Christmas and am still laughed at for my adventure there and the effort to move to Italy then.

Two years ago we decided to go to Northern Italy. I was looking on the internet for apartments in Venice and found a good website offering reasonable rates, I felt. I contacted one owner but he didn't get back to me so I tried another one. This was advertised as being in Veneto, which is the region Venice is in, but it wasn't until later I realised it was actually about a 100 kilometres from Venice, on Lake Garda. The apartment photos looked so good and it had a swimming pool for residents of the apartments, so we decided to give it a try. The owner gave us a good rate with a discount for staying three weeks and offered to pick us up at Treviso airport. We were swayed by all that.

It turned out great, apart from not being in Venice! The owner brought us from the airport to the property, showing us Padua along the way, as she had another property there, which we were offered, if we wanted a change for a week or so. The apartment was about 100 metres from the lake. We were about a kilometre or two outside the town in a nice residential area and a local bus was available to take us into the town if we didn't want to walk. The pool was grand which was just as well as I did not fancy swimming in the lake itself and saw very few, if any, do it. There were nice cafes along the shore near us and hotels and shops, and one internet café where we often ate as well as using their internet. The world cup was on (2006) and Italy won it to our delight. We enjoyed the excitement, but if it had been Ireland there would have been much more. We played tennis in a local sports club indoors! The apartment itself was quite modern and well fitted, including a balcony with a canopy, which we hardly used as we just wanted the sun. The owner was a young business lady and everything was done properly. Our daughter and her boyfriend joined us there for a week and had a good time. They went to Gardaland for a day and had a ball! She went on to au-pair in Via Reggio, near Pisa, and we went down to see her for a day afterwards. We all visited Venice and Verona and one or two of the other towns on the lake. It was all very pleasant. Peschiera Del Garda, the town we were in, is at the southern end of the lake near Verona, and is a beautiful old town with an old historic centre we enjoyed wandering around, but it is not very big.

My wife saw "Immobiliare" (estate agents) offices, of course, and made enquiries, especially when there were just the two of us. A very nice lady showed us some apartments in the town and outside it. We didn't like the ones far out but quite liked the town ones. The town had many advantages, having a hospital, a train station, as well as nice restaurants and other facilities, and no school of English (which interested me greatly, as I felt I could do some business there, maybe even start a school) and being near a motorway which brought one to Venice or Milan. Verona, being so close also attracted me for various reasons, including the possibility of getting work there. It was there we became familiar with terms like bilocale and monolocale (one/ two room apartments or bedrooms) and "Rustico", an old building needing reconstruction, like a farm house or outhouse. We looked a lot and liked the town but saw nothing really to suit us at the right price. But we were learning all the time and becoming clearer on what we really wanted. The viewing trips and talking to agents helped to pass the time pleasantly and varied our days for us. We used them too, just as we offered them opportunities to use us.

The learning curve is important and we were giving ourselves a decent chance of getting the property we wanted in the process. Some people go on a weekend viewing trip and buy off plans or without real thought given to the town or place they arrive in, the difficulties of the not having the language or learning it, the heat of summer or other times of year and many other factors such as socialising, the nature and culture of the people they meet, and so on. Over the years looking, we have often been disappointed for one reason or another and have not always agreed, but it was all worthwhile and I advise people to go through the process and not to act rashly. That is not to say I think I have it all "sussed". I have been to Pizzo many times and I am still finding out much about the place and will continue to do so. It's part of the adventure and enhances the experience. There will be negatives as well as positives also but the negatives can be turned into positives, such as not being able to stay in Pescara, which was a huge disappointment to me, only to keep searching and find Pizzo!

In the last few years, we have both started learning Italian and will continue to do so, out of respect for the country and the people we want to live among and to make it easier for us to get along there, do business and socialise. We had also booked a week of lessons in Pizzo for the end of June, which makes for interesting reading in my diary.

Pescara taught me to be better organised if I want to go live in Italy and to find the right location, not a seaside resort which closes in September. We also have come to the conclusion we may not really want to move here permanently as winters here can be quite cold and wet too. We may want to come for a week or two at that time of year, just for a break, but no more. Two grandchildren have come on the scene in the last two years and, of course we want to see them and be there for them and our children who might still need us from time to time. We have friends and family to keep in contact with and enjoy. We also like Ireland and the life we have created there for ourselves. Donna has her job also which does not allow her to take off for the whole summer and that must be taken into consideration, until she retires, which could be a long way away. There is still a lot to be worked out but here's hoping we enjoy the journey along the way, especially the fine weather and all the other attractions which brought us here.

CHAPTER 3:
The Row_

The scene: Piazza Della Republica, Pizzo, Calabria, Southern Italy

"BASTARDO!!!!!!!"

"You are not nice man, you know the word "gentile" (kind)? ....Well, you not. I give you my time, explain everything you, take trouble, make arrangements, phone people and now……you do this……. bastardo!"

Her words rang in my ears, accusing me. It didn't help that it was not my fault. Yes, I was embarrassed and in public. I didn't bother to reply. It would have been useless. I understood only too well her anger and frustration. I too was furious and very frustrated and very hot. It was high summer in Southern Italy and I should have been enjoying a holiday but instead I was in trouble, being harangued and accused.

She moved away eventually but I still fumed in silence and squirmed. I looked around and faced my wife. The estate agent's words still reverberated around my brain and now I had to say my piece to Donna, whose fault it was, I was in this situation, of course. Of course………

That may have been true subjectively, even objectively, but it didn't make any difference to my beloved and my hopes of sorting this out. It never did. She had other ideas and a different version, I'm sure. I would be the one in the wrong. What's new? But I had never been able to take the advice of a wise man who said "Apologise, say you're sorry …….it doesn't matter whether you did anything wrong or not…just do it….if you want peace or just to survive….."

We had been looking at houses and apartments in Pizzo to buy after our initial visit when we had been entranced. An estate agent couple, Maria and Alessio, had shown us one in the marina and one in the centro storico (old historic town centre). Donna had been excited and interested. She wanted to sign on the dotted line, immediately…….if not sooner. But I was being more cautious, wondering about damp and if there was enough space in the ones we had seen and other considerations. I didn't jump in immediately and agree, which I might have been expected to, because I had been the one pushing for a place in Italy for years.

Because of my doubts, we had gone to the second agent to try to get the low-down on properties in the centro storico. Was damp a problem? Were there other problems? This lady had warned us off and suggested apartments in another area, further along the coast. She suggested we visit them and started to make arrangements. We agreed and were to meet her later as it would take some time to finalise matters. We left her office and went back to the piazza to sit down and get some lunch.

Donna then decided she didn't want to view the properties suggested by the lady agent and said she was tired of the whole thing and had lost interest. I asked her to phone or text, to call the viewing off, but she refused and I had to do it myself, which is why I got an "earful" from the agent when she passed us in the piazza. One row was bad enough but two! I had had enough now.

Skies were so blue you would not expect life could hold any problems but so had the words of the estate agent been and my mood (and that of my wife) was now definitely black and getting blacker. We left Pizzo in silence and took the slow, small, local train back to Tropea, where we had been staying on holiday.

So you may wonder about the name of this book and how we eventually came to buy a property in Italy and in Pizzo too..........and in the centro storico itself.........and why we are very happy about it.

As I said, we had gone first to see an apartment in the marina, down near the beach. It belonged to Toni, who came along eventually, in that very Italian way, which suggests time-keeping is for cretins who don't know how to enjoy life. This attitude is not very far from the Spanish concept of "manana". It is also very Irish according to my foreign students and others but definitely not my attitude. Seemingly an Irish professor of Gaelic was once asked did "manana" have an Irish (gaelic) translation and he opined that it had many but that none suggested "the necessary urgency" involved!

The apartment was on the ground floor of a 3 storey property. It had a front door and a window onto a narrow alley leading down to the beach. It was a 2 bedroom apartment and had recently been fitted out with a kitchen and refurbished. It seemed small and dark to me but appealed to my wife because of its location, being near the marina and beach and it only cost €63,000! I had misgivings but did not verbalise them too much. The next apartment we viewed was in the centro storico, just off the main piazza. It also had 2 bedrooms and seemed much more appropriate and brighter to me. It had no outside space, nor a proper balcony, and provided little opportunity for sun-bathing or getting more sunlight or fresh air. It was up a narrow alley from the Piazza de la Republica and the owner wanted a special arrangement as its purchase because he had bought it less than 5 years before and if he sold it beforehand capital gains tax would kick in. I had no real problem with his suggestions but I wasn't sure about the apartment itself.

So that was how we found ourselves going to the other estate agent and getting advice about damp and other matters such as buying in the centro storico and eventually found ourselves having a row and my wife deciding she was fed up with the whole business and I was accused of being a " bastardo" and not very "gentile"!

We eventually split up for a few hours, me going down to the beach and having a swim and a meal and my wife doing her own thing for an hour or two and eventually joining me down at the marina, where we made our way slowly to the local small train station outside Pizzo, walking slowly and disconsolately and for most of the time apart and me still fuming. Finally, we got the old local, snail train back to Tropea, our dreams seemingly shattered!

CHAPTER 4
Finding The House

We continued our holiday in Tropea, feeling a bit subdued maybe as regards property buying, but still enjoying the beach, the food, the sun and everything Tropea had to offer. When we got home to Dublin, we were still interested in acquiring an Italian property, still captivated by Pizzo, and so we kept in contact with Maria, the estate agent who had shown us properties. She informed us that the one in the marina was sold, and we asked her to let us know if anything interesting came up. I also kept checking her website and saw some that interested me.

On the 24th of July 2007 she let us know about a house on Via Campanella and others for the first time. We contacted her about them and she suggested we should come and view them. We decided to go have a look at them, after us having arrived home only a few weeks previously. We had told her of our general requirements, one or two bedrooms, a sitting room, a kitchen, a balcony or terrace open to the fresh air and the sun, preferably south west facing and not too dear, up to €100,000 or cheaper, but we would consider one which needed restoration. We booked flights, which were expensive enough for us, as it was the summer season and at short notice, and we stayed in a B&B belonging to a man called Felix in Pizzo, whom we later got to know. It was a lovely B&B but expensive enough. It overlooked the cliffs around the corner from the marina and was south-west facing.

We met Maria who showed us an apartment in a block near San Sebastiano, a church up the hill on the way to Via Nazionale with a fine terrace and the aspect we liked. It belonged to a local who had been to America and who also had owned the one we had viewed previously in the centro storico, the one near the piazza. It had antique furniture but was a bit too far from the beach and the centro storico for me. Another one near it was likewise dismissed. Along Via Nazionale, but further from the beach and centro storico, was another fine terraced apartment on the fourth floor. I didn't even go up to view it, as I figured with no lift it would not be a "runner" for a man like me with bad knees.

Then we were shown the old building in Via Campanella, in the centro storico, which was in need of renovation. It was in dire straits but had potential, we thought, and ticked a lot of our boxes. It was near the piazza and not far from the marina. It was part of a bigger house, and could be described as semi-detached with a communal stairs going to the first floor which divided one house from the other. It had its own front door, directly into a living room, and also a door to the dividing stairs. It had a small balcony facing south west and the possibility to open up a terrace. It was advertised as having a kitchen, living room, toilet and store room on the ground floor, with a side entrance also; two bedrooms on the first floor, and also the possibility of a shower room, an angola cottura (small kitchen area), and a spiral staircase to the second floor with a sun terrace. So it was, or could be, a three floor unit, with the option to make separate apartments for renting or having visitors, who could live independently from us, if we were living there, on a different floor. The sun terrace might be a sticking point as permission had to be obtained from the council, a detail not to be taken for granted as it was in the centro storico. If this could be achieved, we would be very interested.

We expressed our desire to purchase the house, if a deal could be worked out, as the asking price was about €55,000 and renovation costs were expected to be about €55,000 also. The realisation that it could be made into two separate apartments because of the external stairs, and thus renting one or both apartments became possible was dawning on us. Or we could live in one and our family or friends could come and stay independently in the other.

There were "cons" as well as "pros" in deciding on buying the house. As it was in the centro storico, which is really a maze of alleys, access was not easy. This makes deliveries and getting work done more difficult, especially during a reconstruction. A car would have to be parked some distance away, but we were not sure we would get one. The house in front of ours has a flat roof, only a few feet above the level of the ground in front of our doorway, but it cannot be built on, we were told, so it seems to give us space and light there. The windows in our house are small and not very plentiful, but some recesses could be reopened as windows, as they were originally, I think. We would buy four walls and a roof for the most part, and it would have to be fitted and furnished. It seemed to be cool in summer but would it need heating in winter and air conditioning in summer? We did not know. Damp worried me but we insisted it be damp-proofed although the owner, our architect and building contractor, was not sure it was needed. Finally, we did worry about having no garden or real outdoor space, which is why we demanded the sun terrace, but it would be possible to sit outside the front and at the side, as Italians do regularly here.

We returned to Dublin and awaited developments. On 9 August we were told contracts could be drawn up as it was expected a terrace would be allowed. Mr Plant, who was the owner of the property, was on holiday however, and we had not got an overall price agreed. On 17 August we were informed the title to the property was in good order and we should get our money sorted as he wanted to go ahead with the sale. But Mr Plant seemed to go missing again and by 4 September we had still no definite news of him. We had arranged to take another holiday anyway in September and not knowing what was happening in Pizzo (or maybe nothing was happening there), we picked another Italian location. It was south of Rome, in Lazio, and would be more reachable from Dublin and also had possibilities as regards property buying. I had been on the internet and discovered the town of Scalea which is also on the sea and had properties which seemed to match our needs. There was a good, lively community of English-speaking people there too, according to the website I found, and an enthusiastic company and group who seemed helpful in the matter of buying property and settling people there. We went to Scauri, a small town near Gaeta and within striking distance of Rome and on a rail line which could bring us to Naples and thus Pizzo.

Scauri was very quiet, but we were quite happy with it. We had a nice apartment, which I had found on a website I often used, and the people were nice too. We holidayed and visited Gaeta, Formia and other places nearby. Eventually Maria got back to us and invited us to view the house in Pizzo again and said we could move on it now. Alessio, who was Maria's partner and an architect and who had checked out the title to the property was at the station in Lamezia Terme to meet us and bring us to Pizzo. He showed us the house on Via Campanella. He surprised us by saying it might be better for us to opt for a new building or one which did not need work on it, as restructuring can pose difficulties and cause heartache. However, we still liked what we saw and said we were still interested and would like to make a deal. So we met Mr Plant, the owner, who was an architect, and also the man who would renovate it for us, if we wished. We talked about the price and how long it would take to do. He had some English but Alessio and himself usually spoke Italian and then Alessio would translate for us. We insisted the deal depended on getting permission for the sun terrace, which Mr Plant assured us he could do. If we were to sign up for it then, we asked, when would it be finished and he replied it could be finished by Christmas!

When we returned home we were told on 26 September that our Italian lawyer had decided that planning permission should be got for the terrace before starting any work. Before that, Mr Plant's plan had been to go ahead regardless, unless someone objected. This permission took some time and we held off agreeing a contract until it came through. On 11 October we were told it was being presented to the Commune di Pizzo, the local authority, along with a notice of commencement of work. It was passed and on 26 October and we were told a notary would send us a contract and Maria would provide a translation for us. It was decision time and we were a bit scared but got some advice from our solicitor in

Dublin who had some Italian and could see nothing wrong with the contract. We went for it and had to send €30,000, we were told, to our bank account in Italy, which Maria had set up for us along with a codisce fiscale (a necessary legality). €7,000 had to be sent to her office in London also. The money was a deposit for the house and an initial payment for the work to begin and would be returned to us if, for any reason, the terrace could not be built. We sent the money and signed the contract. The only problem now was the timescale we were given, which had changed considerably. Mr Plant said he could not start until the end of January on the work and it would be August 2008 before it would be finished. I was not happy with that and let them know. Maria checked it out and said the timescale was reasonable as it was a big, difficult job, but Alessio phoned me and promised me it would be ready for 1 June. I accepted that.

There were other events at the time too, like lots of parties. We even went to a 21st birthday party in Liverpool for my wife's niece and a lot of the family came and had a great weekend. I also had a party for my 60th birthday, which had been planned for months. Family and friends, work colleagues and language group members came along with neighbours and many more. My two sons and their bands provided the music. We danced and drank, ate and talked and a great sing-song ensued after all that. I had been asked by my wife what I wanted and had said a party and I got a good one. My children bought me a laptop and a travelling bag to go with it and both have been very useful, especially here in Pizzo. My younger daughter, the baby of the family got engaged and had a party too, as did my older daughter who had decided to go to Australia for a year. They were all great parties and the social whirl was great. October is the month for birthdays in our family, with three that month. November saw my daughter leave for Australia and she is still there and hoping to stay. It was a tough parting, especially for my wife, who had lost her mother earlier in the year and is still finding it tough now, especially as Frances has met a nice guy there and seems set to stay a while. "Lord, thou art hard on mothers!" As for fathers, we just seem to get on with it, or have to. My wife and I are very happy to see her living life to the full and being happy but separation is tough. It is a time for us again to discover ourselves and maybe indulge ourselves. Pizzo is one answer for me. Hopefully, it will work for my wife too.

CHAPTER 5
Back in Ireland and Signing the Contract

Life was going on in so many other ways too. We are a family of "doers", I think, and as we say in Ireland about nature and personality, our children "didn't pick it up off the stones". I had been involved in a tennis club in Clonee, County Meath, for some time. For the previous two years I had been chairman of the club. In 2006 and 2007 I was head of the planning sub-committee for the new club house. It had been one of my initiatives as chairman and I was very anxious to get it progressed. We had been planning it for two years and had got planning permission and were at the tendering stage in October 2007. We finally had agreed a builder and his estimate and a loan had been arranged. Some wanted to hold off, to try for a lotto grant, which had already been refused, but I wanted to push ahead. At this stage the sub-committee was divided and we were struggling to get attendance at meetings and I was getting more and more impatient and frustrated. I had promised I would stick with it until the end of the year and I did. I reported to the AGM in January and still keep an interest, but with my plan to be away for the summer buying a house in Pizzo and fitting it, I did not think it right for me to stay on any committee and I felt I had done my bit and had informed members I would not be free to continue after 2007. The club house was still not built but I was sure it would be soon and I am glad I walked away from the stress of it all. Christmas came and went, as did New Year's Eve, and my wife and I enjoyed it all with our family, and we looked forward to the year ahead and all it might bring. Maybe next year we would spend it in Pizzo! Work was to begin on our house there at the end of January. An exciting year was in store for many reasons.

Our second son, Bernard, was expecting a baby with his partner, Olive, in March and that was really something to look forward to. We have been very lucky to have Olive and Dermot's partner, Nicola, two wonderfully pleasant, intelligent women with good jobs, come into our lives and enrich them and the fact that we all get on so well is great. Our first grandchild, Lily, was already more than a year old and we often babysat her and loved having her. They had all spent Christmas Day with us and had made it special.

Frances was emailing us every so often from Australia and seemed to be having a good time and had got work out the country there. Mark was working and "gigging" with his bands while Anna was pursuing her studies and heading towards a degree. She was also working at weekends and planning her wedding to Liam, a fine young man, who had gone to the trouble of asking me for her hand in a very polite and maybe traditional way, but it pleased me he had shown respect and a good attitude and he was a hard worker as well. They had known each other since school days and the fact he was interested in football also helped, with me anyway. Anna had picked her wedding reception hotel and we had gone there for Sunday afternoon tea in March to book it and had a lovely meal there on another occasion to celebrate her birthday and my wife's also.

There were worries too. The Camorra in Naples and in Calabria were mentioned in the news now and then and we learned a "Pizzo" was a slang name for protection money and these were not connotations to inspire joy and confidence. Nevertheless, I booked my flight to Naples for 1 June and hoped the house would be ready. Donna would follow me later just in case, and to give me time to sort out difficulties or delays. She does not have extra long holidays and so must arrange and book when she goes on holiday. She did decide to take some unpaid leave also to stay with me longer in Pizzo during the summer and give living in Italy a real go. I started a course in Italian, my third as a beginner, but it was not great, so I eventually chucked it in.

Bernard's baby duly arrived in March as expected and she was healthy and bonny. We were delighted with our new grandchild and Bernard was completely captivated by her and is a great father. Both parents were kept busy as Anna Marie took some time to settle and sleep and it is only now she is not wriggling. A cure for colic or some such from the former Meath GAA manager and famous herbalist, Sean Boylan, did wonders. Both Donna and Olive have great faith in him. Of course, Olive is from his hometown, Dunboyne, the parish where we lived for 17 years, and where Bernard grew up. Meath men like Sean do have some uses and can be special …not that we often like to see them win at Gaelic football, especially if they beat Dublin. I did play football there for about 10 years too and enjoyed it, mostly. They can be tough men too.

We were also in the process of arranging a mortgage and trying to sell a house I owned, which was let. I had bought it soon after I retired from primary school teaching, as an investment and pension. But with the downturn in the market and the difficulty of selling houses in a buyers' market it was not going well. I did get an offer but it was below what I would accept and I refused it. I would continue to let it and hope the prices and the market would stabilise in a year or two. This was all connected as, if I sold the house to let, I would be in a far better position to buy in Italy, without the need for a mortgage. All these matters were consuming my time and my patience and that of my wife, who did not enjoy having to think of them. In fact, she got quite panicky and I had to take on most of the responsibility to alleviate her worries. I felt strong and able for it and she had done the same for me in the past. Her mother's death was still having an effect and she needed time to come to terms with it.

In April I started getting anxious about the progress of our house and emailed Maria about it, only to discover she had thought Alessio was looking after it for us. They were having some relationship problems but he did send me a report and photographs to show the terrace had been opened and the work done thus far was good. I kept at them and wanted more regular reports and photos and was trying to put more pressure on them to have the house finished in time. In May I was informed the next payment of

€48,000 was due and Maria was making arrangements to get an appointment with the notary to complete the sale of the house. I would get the keys at the completion of the sale. Another request came for €15,000 for the hydraulic and electrical work done, another stage payment.

Donna was now having serous misgivings and expressing fears as to how we would get on in Pizzo. She was worried about money also, as there would be little coming in and many expenses to be covered. Our lifestyle there also concerned her. Would we find things to do and people to talk to? We would have to learn Italian or improve our very basic grasp of the language. She was anxious about our family and how they would need us maybe and we would miss them and our grandchildren. All of these are problems and worries which can arise when you are actually facing up to the move to live in a foreign country, even if only for a few months. All I could do was to try and reassure her and remind her of the terrible summer weather we had last year and how she wanted to avoid a repeat and that was why we were going to Pizzo and why we had decided to buy a house abroad. Logic is fine, but feelings and deep emotions were being stirred in her, and logic does not always work so well in such circumstances. I had to be strong in myself also and to exude confidence, even if, at times, I did not feel it. I had a dream and was going to go for it. It was a time to take risks and if I did not do it I would regret it forever. I could and would do it, even at the risk of finding out it did not work out in the end. At least, I would have tried and given it my best. I could do no more.

CHAPTER 6
The Build-up to my Return to Pizzo in 2008

About this time I was really getting excited about the house and feeling good. I also felt inspired to write and find it a good strategy in keeping positive in times of difficulty also. I include it here as it explains my feelings in May of that year before returning to Pizzo:-

"Life couldn't be much better" is what I am feeling on this sunny Sunday morning as I am playing the best tennis I have played for quite some time. It is only social tennis but just getting out on such fine morning is great and playing good tennis is an absolute bonus. I am able to recognise my own good fortune generally and I am especially greatly enjoying delivering winning shots every now and then. What really adds to the whole experience is that I am aware of how happy I am and how grateful I feel to be in this position. Not many people feel this good and admit it and are grateful for it. For me to recognise it is somewhat chastening and maybe unusual, some would say. I am usually assumed to be quite critical, cynical and even negative, according to people I know. Maybe it is to do with the weather and it being sunny. I find that such a help in being upbeat and happy and it is probably why I want to live in Italy.

I have learned to be grateful for life's blessings and this in itself is a blessing and a boon. Some time ago I came across this notion that we should list the reasons why we feel grateful and I have found it useful and fulfilling. Why am I feeling grateful and what is it I am grateful for? Let me list some of my good fortune;-

- I am healthy enough and, having been much worse, I realise how good it feels
- I have been married to a good, beautiful, glamorous wife, who has given me five wonderful children and who has grown with me over 36 years. I am loved and in a loving relationship, which is going well at the present time. As everything has not been perfect always, I am deeply aware of how great that is.
- I love my five children and they love me, I think I can say

truthfully, and I have a good relationship with them for the most part.

- They are healthy, mature, intelligent young men and women making their way in the world and seem to be doing well enough.
- I have no real money worries. I am not as rich as those who are classed as "the wealthy" but I have arrived at a certain stage where money is not the problem it used to be. I am far more comfortable financially than I ever expected to be.
- My home is fine and I have managed to keep it well. It does me and mine fine.
- I need for little, which is a great boon and I find it helps if you don't have huge needs, of all kinds, material and otherwise.
- I live in a nice area and have good neighbours, etc.
- I can play tennis, cycle, swim and partake in life and exercise in a lot of ways.
- I don't do drugs (besides alcohol, which I can control for the most part) or other criminal activities
- I have time to do most of the things I like
- I love travelling, especially to Italy and have been able to do it for a while now
- I have two grandchildren whom I can relate to and enjoy. Their parents are doing well as far as I am concerned and we all get on well.
- The Dermot and Nicola have bought a house recently and the others have a house and all have good jobs.
- My youngest daughter, Anna, is engaged to a good, sensible man (and they are to marry in 2009.. and they did). She is still at college but they are doing very well as regards accommodation, material goods, career and other areas. They are full of plans and I admire their ambitions and "can do" attitude.
- My other daughter, Frances, is in Australia and "having a ball" by all accounts. She and I get on much better now and she is doing well in her career and life, as well as in Australia.
- My other son, Mark, is very happy playing in his band, living

in Temple Bar and holding down a job which does for him what he wants it to do.

- I have had a good life mostly.
- I can afford a car, computer, holidays, etc.
- My family of origin are good people (but some are now in ill health) and so are their families. We get together every so often and get on well enough.
- I can get along with life despite its difficulties. I am a survivor
- I have a soul, an inner life and a personality I can live with. I like poetry, songs, art, and can appreciate beauty in its many aspects, eg nature, people, music etc.
- I am Irish and can speak the language and love and enjoy the best of the culture
- I am a moral person but not perfect.
- I have somebody to talk to and share with.
- My summer holidays start soon and I am off to Italy to complete a house deal there and to enjoy the whole summer there. It will be an adventure and the realisation of a dream I have had for a long time. My wife and I have been learning Italian and plan to go to classes when we get there next month.

Of course, I didn't think of every one of these things this morning when I felt life was good but I thought of many of them and have considered them all before and found writing this list beneficial and therapeutic, now and previously.

Just in case you think this is all a bit smug, let me state I am not always deliriously happy and indeed I have had lots of problems, lots of regrets and unfulfilled dreams. Death has been an unwelcome visitor both to my own family and to my family of origin. We have had our share of sickness, trouble and strife. I personally have had my own health problems, which were problems for my wife and family also, of course. I don't bother too much with materialism, have not had fantasies about driving a Ferrari or a Maserati but it would have been nice to have a BMW, Mercedes or a Rover even! A home in Dublin 4 would have been great too but "so what!?" When we were getting married in the seventies, my wife and I visited the usual new housing estate in a very working class area of Dublin and, to her surprise, I declared I wasn't interested in living there, but it was basically like where we have ended up, but a bit better, as far as I am concerned! Many things did not work out and I have learned to live with the relative disappointment and get on with life, and maybe be no "great shakes".......but no, I am not smug and full of myself. My teaching career was very ordinary, if interesting, and I did not get to be principal of a school and develop things along the lines I wished. Life has not been the proverbial "bowl of cherries" and some ill health and a degree of doing-without has been my lot sometimes. On a lighter note, I never got to have the football career I craved as a kid. Somehow, I did not get to play for Ireland in soccer, not even for Shamrock Rovers, the team I followed in my youth! In fact, I got to play very little organised soccer and certainly not with any great success but I enjoyed what I did do. Likewise, I never managed to play for Dublin in Croke Park or for Waterford hurlers. I never even managed to play in Croke Park, Dalymount or Lansdowne Road at all! As this chapter has started on such a positive note I would like to keep it up so I will not detail all the miserable moments to prove how tough it has been at times. There is no need. Everybody has had such moments. It is how you deal with them that matters.

I prefer now to dwell on the good I have experienced and how well I feel and I am extremely thankful for it all and intend to go on like this, even to the extent of taking risks like buying a house in Italy to enjoy life and all that sunshine, sea, food, history and the whole wonderful Italian experience. I am not willing to "gently into that good night" just yet!

The whole business of buying a house in Italy really started to kick in now, a few weeks before I was to go. We were going to have to complete the purchase of the house with the official, the "notaio" (notary public), and a date was fixed for 3 June in Pizzo. I was going to be there then but Donna was not, so I had to get a power of attorney form signed officially for her at the Italian Embassy in Dublin in order that I could act for her, as well as myself. We found the embassy and did the business without too much trouble.

Then Maria asked us to make a decision about a wall on the first floor which was in the original plan. If it was erected as planned, it would not allow us much space in the front room. We had planned to have a bedroom there and it would not be able to take a double bed with such a placement of the wall, according to Maria. Unfortunately also, if we did take the other option to place the wall differently, we would have the spiral staircase in the bedroom, which was not great. Decisions! Decisions!

It is very hard to make such decisions from a distance of hundreds of miles with only a plan to go on but we opted to take her advice and change the position of the wall. We could always change later or put up a partition to separate the room from the spiral staircase which accessed the second floor. The irony is that when we went to Pizzo we changed our minds about the use of that room and decided to make it into a second living room. It was so bright, in contrast to the one below and had a balcony with big doors opening to allow light and air in and we were quite happy to do so but the worry about the double bed was for nought!

A form to allow Maria access to my money account had been posted but had not arrived for a few weeks and so everything would have to wait until I got there to withdraw money and pay everybody. We had to pay for the house itself, the services of the notaio, the local taxes, my agent's fee and the payments due for works done. It was all adding up and we had to keep our nerve.

There were many other happenings at that time also. Bernard and Olive invited us to a BBQ in their house in Kentstown and most of the family went and we met most of her family. The christening of Anna Marie, their daughter, was set for a week later so we all met up again and had a great time on both occasions. The sun shone for a few weeks, just as it had done the previous May (and in June it rained for a month again, just like last year). We watched the rugby match in which Munster won the Heineken Cup and also Ireland's soccer game against Slovenia with Trappatoni in charge.

Dermot was busy getting his house refurbished and Anna was doing her exams. Dermot had some problems getting things done and had to move in with us for a while afterwards as the house was basically "gutted" and unsafe for Nicola and Lily, who found it "tough going". They also had to go to Waterford for a few days to escape the worst of it.

I was counting down the days to flying to Naples and had decided to have a BBQ for all the family, if the weather allowed, on the day before I went. The weather held out and my sister joined us as well as my own family. I even went and bought and assembled a new BBQ appliance on the Saturday morning and also used the old pot-type one, just to meet a challenge which Olive had put to me the week before. It all worked and I drank too much and had a great day, but maybe it was not the best preparation for a long day travelling on the morrow. Things were really humming during those weeks and despite the pressures of getting everything ready and finishing up work for the summer, which can be wearying, I felt good. Donna was not so sure about it all and I had to be confident for both of us. I would miss her for the two weeks also but I hoped to get things moving faster and have the house ready as soon as possible.

So on that Saturday night, after our BBQ, I packed my bag as best I could and set the clock for 3.30am. My wife drove me to the airport. It felt strange not travelling with her, with her minding my passport and my being attentive to her also, as we usually did, but I managed, as I had done 36 years ago before we got married. Yes, it was probably the first time since then that we had flown apart! The flight was not noteworthy and I landed in Naples about 11.30am local time. I had time to have lunch and relax as my train did not depart until after 3pm. The heat got to me and already I was sweating. The ticket office had been changed and I had some difficulty finding it and the right platform and I did worry slightly. The worst that happened was that I almost lost my computer and the trolley bag I had it in when I forgot it at the ticket desk and had to rush back from a shop where I was buying some cold water. What a relief to find it still there and not stolen, in Naples station, of all places!

The train journey was about four hours long and the train was packed but I had a ticket and a seat booked, thanks to Alessia in Maria's office. The next day was a public holiday in Italy, in honour of the republic and many people were travelling so it was just as well I had managed to get a booking. At Vibo-Pizzo station I got a taxi into Pizzo. I had arrived at last!

Tropea and it's iconic convent on a rock jutting into the sea

Donna and myself at a beach café in Tropea

Looking down from the piazza and south out to sea

Our first view of Pizzo: the promenade, the cliffs and town above them

The peaceful piazza in the daytime sun ...
"It must be the mezzogiorno!"

Donna, my wife, in the sea at Tropea beach

Donna outside the “rustico” house before it was renovated

The ground floor room completely “fitted out”
…….. to Donna’s distress

The condition of the front wall suggested damp problems, to say the least

Another view of the ground floor

Old roof beams painted white which were stripped back, varnished and re-used

The old toilet ..beautiful white tiles and running water!

Front of first floor room and balcony ....in its original state

The first breakthrough into the roof and front wall
to make the terrace

The old roof revealed; replaced with new roof and tiles, but with old beam

The old shed at the back had to be dug out to a depth which revealed these pipes!

Two new floors had to be constructed,
lowering the previous ceilings

Ground floor room inner wall broken through to back shed;
(our new sitting room and kitchen accessed through a new arch)

Front view of house from below

Back room window on first floor, looking out on tree in next door garden

CHAPTER 7

"A melancholy yearning for the glow

Of spring-times past, of warm and festal eves,

When here in the piazza used to dance

The beauteous women,"

Giosue Carducci

June Diary

SUNDAY 1 JUNE 2008

The Piazza Della Republica is crowded, more than anytime last year when I was here, and a festival spirit is in the air. My taxi driver is just about allowed into the piazza after begging the local traffic wardens.

I sit myself down in front of the Pantheon Bar, one of my favourite haunts in Pizzo, and take in the scene. Children are arranging flowers petals in a corner over near the church, making some image, religious no doubt. My bar host approaches and I order my first beer of the holiday. He enquires "Grande?" and I get the feeling he remembers me. I am at home, but on my holidays!

A bride and groom sweep by, to applause and cheering. It is like something in a Fellini film. There are loud bangs from somewhere and a multitude of swallows fly about. Some young man near me shouts something racy, or just funny maybe, to the married couple and there is general laughter. Someone else says "I give them two months". I text my daughter, who is going to be married next year, about the bride and groom and she texts back to say she is dying to come and see it all, especially the just-married couples who often parade thus in Pizzo. We wanted her to get married in Italy and have all this but she wants her friends and family at home and she will get what she wants. I text my wife and she just replies that she is jealous. I have come earlier than her to get the house completed on time and to make sure it is ready. That was the plan anyway.

There are church bells ringing, young macho bikers revving their machines, lovers strolling arm in arm, couples kissing, drivers having rows, older men sitting, drinking, smoking and talking. It is in the cool of the evening after a hot day. The young studs and "femme fatales" add colour and brio to the piazza. More tables are spreading farther into the piazza than I ever remember. A band suddenly emerges and belts out music providing the soundtrack and completing the scene. I have arrived at a very good time. "What a welcome!" Ok, it's not for me but I take it as a personal welcome, an endorsement and a good omen and it is "magnifico".

It had been a long day. The day before was great but it had not helped. I had invited my family and my sister to a BBQ and the weather had obliged. That morning we got up early as I had to buy food and a new gas BBQ. Our old charcoal would be used too, but it was no longer enough. However, I had determined to use it, as Olive the partner of Bernard, our second son, had challenged me to use it on the occasion of the christening of their daughter, Anna Marie, the week before! So we bought the new one and I spent most of the morning assembling it and finding out how to use it. The BBQ worked out great, including the old one, which I cooked on, and my sister said she preferred the food cooked on it. So there, Olive! (only joking). It was a great day and I drank too much and had to pack my case at 9pm that night and try to get some sleep before arriving at the airport at about 5 pm!

The flight had been fine and then I got the local bus into Piazza

Garibaldi in Naples as I had plenty of time before my train at 15.22. Eventually, I found the right ticket office and platform, almost losing my computer and a small case, as I got so frustrated talking to the official in the office and went off with my big case and without the smaller one. Buying water at a kiosk a minute later, I realised my mistake and ran back to find it still there! In Naples! What a break! The train was crowded, it being a bank holiday weekend and next day was Republic Day in Italy. I arrived into Vibo-Pizzo station at about 19.45 and got my taxi to Pizzo.

So here I was. I looked around for people I had met last year but did not see them. Now I had to find Mr. Plant, owner of the B&B where I was to stay, and vendor of the house I was buying. He was also the one managing its reconstruction and so a very important man for me. I went to the B&B and met him there almost immediately. It was great to get into clean clothes and to have found my place to sleep. What a relief, after the long day and night!

I heard a choir singing next. There is more to this welcome. I rushed out to taste to the full the enchantment. Bells are ringing again and a procession is taking place. It is a religious festival I have chanced on and the band reappears followed by priests, one holding the gold monstrance with the Blessed Sacrament inside, and a retinue of followers, many in soutanes and other robes, of various colours. They say prayers and then the fireworks start. It is all a colourful spectacle and I take some photos. Later, going to look at the house I am buying I see lanes decorated with flowers and canopies, petals strewn on the ground and an altar erected in one place. The procession had come along this route and so the residents had done their best to enhance the streets. There were strong feelings of community evident which made feel optimistic I was buying in a wonderful place.

MONDAY 2 JUNE

Sleeping until 5.30, I woke to bird song and first light. I had left a window open and just closed it and went back to sleep! (So much for romantic ideas of the dawn and the beauties of bird song). Eventually I arise at 10.30, shower, and go view my house. There are workers there mixing cement or plaster and it shows there is a pressure to get it finished, I suppose, as this is a public holiday in Italy, Republic Day. There are piles of wood, stones, old pipes and other stuff outside, which have obviously been removed from the house. Inside it is a mess but I try the ladder to the sun terrace we demanded and it gives me a view over the sea, which is what we wanted as well as an outsider area with fresh air and natural light, open to the sun. I take photos to send home, just to prove it. There seem to be lots of not very big rooms but the state of the place makes me very suspicious as to the **real** completion date (1 June, I had been told by Alessio) . I take some more photos and go for a cappuccino and cornetto (croissant).

Getting back to my B&B, I set up my computer and realise I need an adaptor as the one I find in my baggage does not work. I rush out before lunchtime closing and the mezzogiorno (midday) and manage to purchase the correct one. Now for the internet, which is when I remember what Alessia, in Maria's office told me; I would need to purchase a card or internet key from TIM or WIND. Asking around, I am almost laughed at……"There is no such internet device in Pizzo" seems to be the attitude. I tried the tabacchi, as well as an agency of some kind and was told to go to the tourist office, but it was closed. Tomorrow might bring more luck. So it was time for lunch and a "Rustico" (panino type) and beer would fill the gap. The guy I had seen yesterday, who was from the tourist office in the piazza, walked by and I asked him about internet connections but he did not know, although he was trying to be helpful. Another snack might help, so I tried "Polpetta di carne", a pulped meat item, which went down well enough.

"Music hath charms to soothe the (savage) breast" so I went back to my abode and listened to it on my computer, feeling like a bit of a prat about the internet. Then I got myself organised to go for a swim and went down the stairs to the road, when the lady in the flat below came out to check me out. Off to the beach I went, down all those steps from Piazza Della Republica, which had made me think of buying a scooter since last year because of my bad knees. So I had my swim anyway and got to texting my wife and others. (It was then I decided on this diary or book idea .. I hope it works for me .. and you.)

The beach was becoming crowded with bank holiday crowds converging. Bikers arrived and the new train-like small bus for tourists and children made its appearance to shouts and welcomes. I had an ice cream and prosecco to pass the time pleasantly. Then it was back up those steps, passing an apartment we had looked at last year. Toni's place I had considered just too dark and small for me, but it seemed occupied now.

Reflecting later on, I wondered would this work for us, Pizzo and the house we were buying. Another idea floated into my brain, "Could I get accommodation while waiting for the house to be completed, in exchange for English lessons?" Other such ideas such as just teaching for fees were entertained. I had no books with me, however, and decided I would try out Vibo-Valentia, a bigger shopping town nearby. Maybe I would get my internet connection there too.

The Italians are great strollers, especially in the evening, walking along in great style, often all dressed up and having their ice cream. They crowded the marina and the piazza. The sun came out and overcast skies cleared and reappeared every so often. There was the odd row too, as emotional Italians will engage in such. A guy with a pizza wants to get back in the train/bus but is not allowed. His lady friends or relatives pull him away and peace is restored. Not everybody is happy in Pizzo, always.

On my way back to the apartment I call into the Pantheon Bar where I get "slagged" for being red-faced with the sun. I am embarrassed (or "scarleh (t)" , as my former pupils might have said). My wife also talks about "lobsters", red-skinned or sunburnt people she sees after a sunny day in Dublin. It is 8pm and dusk is setting in. I drink a prosecco instead of beer, in the hope of, at least, not adding to my girth. I am reminded of the hotel owner in Fiuggi outside Rome who suggested I should drink wine instead of beer. I also decide I don't need a full dinner every night, that a snack might do sometimes. But will it work as regards losing weight?

"Devo mangiare pizza a Pizzo" (I must eat pizza in Pizzo), I try to pun, in my beginner's Italian.
"Pizza" she replies, seemingly not over-impressed with my extensive command of the language.

A girl drives up to the bar and waits while her male partner goes into it. She looks around at the young men sitting eating and doesn't move a bit, even when "beeped" by a car behind for blocking the narrow passageway. She is coolness itself, waiting for her man to get the food in. What confidence and calm! Whatever it is, she has it. Some people might say she is unresponsive, uncaring, but were I or other Irish people in her situation we would be either too accommodating or start a row, I think. Maybe we are too nice for our own good, some of us.

The culture of eating out is different too. Whole families eat out together, teenagers and children included, even at night. There is little bad behaviour unlike some Sunday pubs I have been in where children run around madly while their parents drink and don't seem to notice. The young girls are mostly thin as rakes and usually have striking features. How do they turn into typical Italian "mamas", small and squat often, though not always?
Pasta and focaccia may take its toll. The crowds thin out as the night wears on and there is a flow and ebb to the life.

The Italians I see are lively and good-humoured, not like the ones Paddy Agnew describes when he went to Rome at first. His book,

"Forza Italia", which I am reading, is, like his column, highly entertaining and readable. It is about football and his moving to Italy to live, both of which I am very interested in. The life here seems different to Rome or that part whereof he writes; people here walk about at night, stay outside longer, eating, drinking, smoking, talking, gesticulating, gesturing and posing . Others watch the passing parade from balconies or preparing their meals. They are really alive, taking part in one way or another; not stuck inside, whether at home watching tv or in a pub, the Irish way. It is still warm outside and much more "stimulante" and "interessante", to me anyway.

Then I hear singing and it interests me greatly but I have just ordered a beer and by the time it arrives and I get to where the music came from, it stops. I am disappointed.

TUESDAY 3 JUNE

Today was the day I had to sign for the house and I finally get to own it. I had been up all night worrying about all sorts of things………..did I have the documents? Why hadn't I brought my Pizzo file from home? Why couldn't I get through to Maria by texting? Would she be there in the morning and at what time?

Maria did turn up about 9 am, startling me as I was reading "Teacher Man" by Frank McCourt, to distract myself from my worries, while having my cappuccino in the piazza. We went to Catanzaro, to the bank where I had sent money from Ireland, Maria having set up an account for me there months ago. We went straight in, after the usual (for the non-Italian) hair-raising drive through narrow alleys with cars driving past you in the opposite direction. Maria knocked on an official's door and we got straight to work, after the usual introductions. Ida, for she was our bank official, had all the papers ready and soon I had an ATM card and had activated it with Maria to get our statement. The money I had sent from Ireland had arrived thankfully. Bank drafts for various payments to the vendor, the notaio, and Maria herself were produced and cash to pay for work on the house. Many forms were signed and we were out of there in about half an hour amazingly. All had gone well as opposed to many bureaucratic nightmares I had read about in Italy. Of course, about €70,000 had been deducted from my account, but if you want to buy a house you have to pay, even in Calabria, I guess.

We had orange juice outside a pavement café and discussed other business we had in common and, before going, I asked about getting my laptop connected to the internet by means of a Wind card or some such device. Maria tried for me in a Vodaphone shop where the assistant produced a USB style device but it was not successful in the end and we decided to leave it for the present.

Coming back from Catanzaro, we talked about property in Ireland, England and Italy and the general state of the economy worldwide and other topics which arose. When we got to Pizzo we arranged to meet Mr Plant and had a look at the house. The workers left for lunch and handed me the keys to lock up! The old metal balcony had been removed from the window on the first floor and scaffolding had been erected since I had seen it the day before. Mr Plant's brother, Francesco, arrived and Maria had a chat with him, which seemed to suggest it would not be ready for occupation when Donna, my wife, came on 14 June. However, Maria was not sure he was up to date on the progress of work and we went to lunch and waited for Mr Plant to arrive.

At lunch they talked and it became clear Mr Plant was adamant the house could not be occupied by us before the end of June, even into July, but Maria held him to a date at the end of June. I would have to find accommodation from Saturday 7 June for myself and from 14 June for Donna also. I had thought of offering English lessons in exchange for English lessons and Maria was going to help me or try to find a reasonably cheap apartment for me/us to rent for a few weeks. Mr Plant offered his mother's apartment for a reasonable sum and I agreed to have a look at it.

Lunch being over, and our next meeting not due until 3pm I asked Maria if she had anything else to do as I wanted to have a "kip" or just relax for an hour or two. She was glad to get some free time, I think, and we agreed to meet at the car park about 2.45pm. I wrote up some stuff on the laptop, read a bit and cleaned myself up to relax. We met up and went to the notaio's office. Maria wanted to go in to have a look at the documents but the notaio was not in. We waited outside at a café table for the notaio and Mr Plant and his entourage. Half an hour later the notaio's secretary arrived and then Mr Plant, Francesco his brother, and Signore Sardinelli, who acted as agent for Mr Plant in selling the house.

When we went into the office Maria got straight to work, asking if an English translation of the document was available and was not pleased to get a negative answer. She was also told the notaio's office did not have the internet or even mobile phone facilities. She wasn't sure if this were true or the secretary was just being awkward. Waiting for the notaio delayed matters again and this set the tone of the meeting, which lasted much longer than usual, it seems. When the notaio did arrive there were more introductions but she was business-like and much discussion, some very animated, followed. It was all in Italian and so I did not understand it but knew there was some important markers being laid down. Every so often Maria would let me know what was involved or I would ask her a question. For the most part I was quiet and calm as there was not much I could do but trust Maria and the notaio to ensure I was being fairly treated. Various groupings retired to another room from time to time to hammer out an English translation or discuss terms. Eventually, Maria came back with a rough English draft and the notaio read out the terms of the deal in Italian while Maria showed me the English version simultaneously. Alterations and additions were made and then there was another delay before we all signed the documents and I got the rough draft with a promise to get a proper finished document, which I could collect in about 30 days time at the office. Cheques were handed over and Maria showed Mr Plant an agreement for further works on the house which we also signed. She had to rush off to collect her children and Mr Plant brought me to see his mother's apartment and I agreed to take it. I also handed him some cash for the work he had already done on the house. Almost 3 hours later we were finally finished the business and I felt relieved that it was all over. I had intended going to Tropea to hear a singer that night but on checking train times in the tourist office I realised it would be too tight to get there, listen to the singer and get back so I just went for a beer and later some dinner.

I texted Donna with the news almost immediately and invited her to phone me which she did about half an hour later. She was pleased and hoped I was ok. She was trusting me to do whatever I had to do and make decisions about matters. She had her own news of home and how she wasn't getting as much time on her own as she had expected but she was fine. Dermot and Bernard and their partners and children had been with her and all was ok. I was not to sound too happy on my own, she said, but she was glad for me.........I think!

WEDNESDAY 4 JUNE

I am going to Vibo to try sort out internet connection and maybe get an Italian phone. On the way up the hill to the bus stop I pass our house and take some photos. There is scaffolding going up and one of the twins is working on it. All the windows and doors have been removed (one reason why we cannot move in) and I take a photo of a view over our new roof towards the sea.

There were no bus tickets to be got in Pizzo, although it is advertised outside a kiosk, for instance, but I am told to get them on the bus itself. There are great views out to sea and over the coast from the bus and it calls at Vibo-Pizzo train station, which could be useful in future. When I get to Vibo it is raining and I walk around getting drenched. I call into a café for cappuccino and to enquire about where I might get a phone and/or a device for internet connectivity, like a TIM or WIND card, as Alessia in Maria's office had suggested. I am sent to a phone centre but it is for making calls to far-off homelands. I go into the supermarket and ask and am given more directions I don't follow or understand but eventually I find a Vodaphone shop.

The assistant has no English and I feel I need to use it as my Italian is not good enough for buying what could be an expensive item and I need to get it right. She calls on another staff member who has English and he suggests a Vodaphone internet key. He says it is the only way to do it. First I must buy the SIM card, like for a phone, then connect it to the internet key and insert it like a USB cable in my laptop. It will be €200 to buy and then it costs €30 for 100 hours of use. He tries it in my laptop but it does not work. He is amazed and suggests something is wrong with my laptop, which I am not inclined to disagree with as two danger notices come up from Norton Protection Software. I buy a cheap Italian phone and leave. The next stop is an internet point where I send my first emails of the holiday and it lashes rain outside. Tired, wet and frustrated, I find a lovely modern restaurant offering snacks and a full range of lunch food. My food is very good and cheap and I have a beer. There is a bus stop opposite but a bus sails past me, the driver waving his finger at me and indicating I am at the wrong stop. I go back to the restaurant and am told I need to go around the corner to find the correct bus stop for Pizzo. I make enquiries there and a school girl of about 16 years of age assures me I am in the correct spot. We get talking. It is the last day of school before the summer holidays. She does not love school at which I laugh, telling her I am a teacher. She lives in Marinella, a seaside resort outside Pizzo, which I have heard about. I ask her will she work for the summer and she laughs a "No". She will dance and relax. This is a wise girl.

I have a tv in my B&B and realise I haven't turned it on since I came. I still don't and I don't think we will get one for the house. I take it easy for the rest of the day and am back in my B&B at 8 pm. This is really getting ridiculous. I am not even drinking or eating much. I had lunch in yesterday, just fruit, prosciutto crudo and acgua frizzante! The simple life is catching!

THURSDAY 5 JUNE

Not being able to sleep late, I got up at 7am to write until about 9am. Then I took myself off to have breakfast in the piazza, where I did Sudoku and wrote some postcards to family, colleagues and friends before going to the internet point on Via Nazionale. I sent emails and some photos and some of my writing to my wife and children. I enquired about the Italian school we have enrolled in from 30 June but nobody knew about it at the school near Bar Amici.

I have been trying my "Poco Italiano" (a little of the Italian language), and enjoying doing it. I have even been stopped on the street by Italians looking for places and have answered

" Sono di Irlanda. Non io so." (I am from Ireland, I don't know), the latter a very important phrase in any language.

I made enquiries about a scooter and was told I could get one, secondhand, for about €2000 or to hire for about €300 a month, including helmet, insurance etc. I decided to wait until my wife arrives before doing either.

Then back to the piazza, to another bar (I am giving them all some custom, not to offend any) where I comment to the girl "Lavora sempre?" (always working) but she does not rise to my bait. With the sun shining and me having ice cream and reading a good book, "Teacher Man" by Frank McCourt, I am not too worried. I finish it, loving the extras at the end like the interview with him, his list of favourite books etc, and am sad it is over. A good read is hard to find, as my wife puns. Her surname is Reid, and she usually describes herself as "A good read in bed", ... far too modestly!.

Getting my laptop connected to the internet is something I want to do and a girl, Carmen, in a local phone shop tells me to come back tomorrow and she will help me. Then it is back to my B&B to write in the mezzogiorno (midday) and I also want to set up my digital frame (for photos), which I got from my children as a going away present. By 4.30pm I have had enough and the sun is shining brightly so it is off to the beach with me. There was nobody else there apart from a couple, kissing and holding hands. I undress and keep watching them, feeling jealous. She seems to be urging and encouraging him, maybe to commit, and I want to tell them it will be ok. Eventually they leave and I feel I am the gooseberry, sadly. When Donna and I went to the film "Once" we were the only ones in the cinema in Blanchardstown and a single guy came in just before the start and sat down right beside me. "What a plonker", were my thoughts, in the immortal words of Del Boy. He definitely played the gooseberry, but why? One can only surmise.

I had a cool swim, getting into my depth very quickly, which I like. I swam, floated and completely relaxed, the only one in the water. "Life is good" I thought and I felt wise thinking it and about myself. I was "living the dream" as my daughter had said to me in a text. I walked up and down the beach, picked up a stone which took my fancy. There and then I decided to collect one every time I went for a swim. I found a pumice stone which intrigues me for some reason, and I remember some poetry which mentions pumice that I had learned for my Leaving Cert in 1966. I feel I am getting life right. It is so easy to get caught up in materialism and worry. What I have now is "it", as far as I am concerned. It is not always possible to maintain it, the peace and contentment I feel, but I have to go for it. I am not eating or drinking too much, which I also take as a sign of my new equilibrium.

Observing the scene, I see three boats out at sea, with three rings of nets or some such and I wonder is it for fish-farming. I want to ask someone but there is no one to ask. I must try sailing, as I said I would, and find an instructor with English as my Italian is not good enough. Things to do, "Promises to keep, and miles to go, before I sleep"! My Italian pronunciation needs attention too, I know. Is it "Stromboli", with an emphasis on the first syllable or the second one, which I see (or even cannot see)? Do I need a lavanderia, with a long "e" sound or a short one? Such thoughts make me feel I am on the proverbial "busman's holiday". Teachers!

Later, in the piazza where I eat and drink, a child picks a flower and a mother, I think, smiles, sharing the moment with him, love and happiness spreading across her features. My "Panino Superbo" is just that, with salsiccia piccante, cippola, mozzarella, n'djou, and all for only €4! Old men argue about something, everything, living through their animated talk. They may have no jobs as there is little industry and employment here but they know how to live and survive here. It is not easy for them, I am sure. There is heated debate about the bus/train for tourists maybe, but it is just something to get excited about and display one-up-man-ship and the competitive spirit, shouting each other down. There is an older teenager, who constantly cycles around, gets into fights with others and now and then does odd jobs for shopkeepers and bar persons. There are gangs of young students outside a shop on their last day in school before the holidays or maybe on a school trip. The owner tries to keep an eye on them and they jostle and shout, in high spirits. They remind me of so many occasions like this in which I was involved, making me feel quite at home. One leers at a sexy lady with an older man. Is he lusting after her himself? The girls are quieter, standing on the outside of the group, hoping to be noticed. Some are in groups clicking together and excluding others ("You are my friend today!"). Teachers and/or parents hover, keeping order. A teacher comes and wants to play the fuzzball. Now there is crack! Holidays can be an anti-climax for some students. "It is holiday time..we must go mad…it's not happening..I'm bored already and it's only beginning!" There is a younger child with a gun of some kind which shoots "bullets". His father is watching him but takes the gun and tries a shot and then warns the child not to shoot at the head or higher up! The students are finally gathered together and marched off. I decide I don't need a real dinner after all. I am sated for the day.

VENERDI 6 GIUGNO

Today I decided to revisit last year's holiday place, Tropea, for many reasons. I wanted to take a break from Pizzo, see old haunts, meet Cettina (somebody we got to know last year, who worked in the estate agents trying to sell us apartments in Palazzo Tropea). I really wanted to go later in the day but when I called into the phone shop in Pizzo, where Carmen had told me to return to get my internet connection sorted I was told I would have to come back at 6pm. She sold me a Sim card first and said I would have to activate it later, before coming back, by phoning the company to register it in some way. I wasn't sure about all this and if it would work and kept asking "Certamente?" but she seemed sure enough and I really wanted to get internet connectivity. The Sim card cost €10 and she said I would get 100 hours of internet for €30 a month with the card! It seemed so much cheaper than the key and I decided to go for it.

"Take risks" my new mentality said to me.

"Yeah, wait and see what happens!" says my old one.

Then I asked her about a bus to Tropea and was told to take the train. I was later than I wanted to be, as I knew things would close in Tropea at 1pm, but I had to be back in Pizzo for 6pm, so I decided to go.

The station is a bit of a walk from the centro storico but when I got there I was happy enough to learn a train would be along in about

30 minutes. I sat down and did some writing and waited. There was no ticket office open so when the train came I just jumped aboard. Of course, I was asked to pay by the train official and thought I had annoyed him by not having the ticket or change for the fare but he wrote my ticket and came back with change later. He was helpful, telling me the times of the return train and again I am amazed by the warmth of the people, even officials, who have got a bad press often in Italy. It helps that I try my Italiano with them, I suppose also.

Getting into Tropea before 12.00 meant I had little over an hour to do any business, such as go on the internet, drop in to Cettina, and buy a t-shirt and get “Sono Pizzitano” inscribed on it. “Two out of three” ain’t bad as the song says. I called into Cettina in her office where we often sat last year when we were thinking of buying in Tropea. The apartments in the Palazzo were not finished and by the sound of her there were problems. Still, she seemed glad to see me and was suitably surprised. We had a few minutes before I said I had to go to the internet point before it closed. She offered to let me use her internet if I could not get all my business done in time but she was not free for lunch, so I promised her that Donna and I would call other some day during the summer. I rushed off to the internet point and got on my own computer there, but connected to the internet by their LAN. It suited me better but I still had to rush to get everything done. I had written my email already and had it and attachments ready on my memory stick. It was great but I had much more to do and wanted to send my main email to Donna and all the children and also send her a private one. I emailed Maria and Nausicaa, the school we had booked into for Italian lesson last January. I checked my internet banking and finally finished a few minutes before 1pm. The owner had been interested in buying in Palazzo Tropea also so I asked him how it was going and he let me know there were problems. Wasn’t I glad we had opted out! I told him about our buying in Pizzo and left quite happily.

Now I could visit the places I had been in Tropea and had wanted to see again. Top of the list was my favourite bar and I made my way to Café de Paris and looked for another Franco. I found him but he didn't seem to remember me. I had a "birra grande" anyway and his waiter certainly remembered me. There was no crack to be had, however, so I moved on to get some food and tried a new bar for me, one with pizza and other snacks. The piccante pizza was excellent and the second beer went down well too. Next, I felt like going back to where we had had an apartment to rent and along by the old Norman church, which I tried to get Anna to marry in next year, as well as the restaurant we frequented most in Tropea, but all was very quiet. I did ring the bell of the owner of the palazzo we had stayed in, but got no answer. My wanderings continued around Tropea but it was the Mezzogiorno (midday: a time when little happens and also a concept or attitude and a name given to southern Italian parts probably by those from the north who feel superior: this is surmise: may also be compared to the Spanish Siesta) and there was little activity. Of course, I had to view the beaches but didn't go down to them and made sure to see the convent on the huge rock jutting out into the sea. It was still magnificent but Tropea had not lived up to my memories and I decided to get an earlier train back. There is not much point in being there in the Mezzogiorno, the sleepy part of the day and, seemingly, whoever said, "you should never go back!" was right.

Tired and hot, I trudged up the streets to the station and again from Pizzo station back to my B&B. I wanted to get my internet connected and Carmen, that helpful girl in the phone shop, had told me to phone TIM to get it going, but neither Cettina nor I had been able to. I quickly showered, as I was not the best, and set off again for the shop to meet Carmen. She had told me to return at 6 pm but I figured I needed her to activate the TIM Sim card and so I turned up early. The shop did not open at 4 pm as most did, so I had to wait around. My Italian phone was not working either and I did try to get people to help but to no avail. I found the shop open at 5pm and Carmen there, thank God (I didn't want to have to explain myself all over again). She calmly took charge of the situation and activated my phone and my TIM Sim card. Then she asked me for my USB connection to the phone or some such device. I didn't have one and she explained to me I should have got one with my phone. So I asked her did she have one to sell and she did. It only cost €179 and the penny dropped! This did make a difference but it made sense. The internet key the man in Vibo had tried to sell me cost €199. I hadn't really expected to get away with a card for only €30 a month without paying something like €180 or €200 for a device, like the key, to connect me to the internet. Well, it would have been nice but I paid up and she went to work. She put a lot into it and her colleague also and eventually it was installed and the language changed to English and then she had to go. I would have to return tomorrow to await a message from TIM and finalise the operation. Her colleague finished the job and sorted out my package and then asked for the money. I was still apprehensive but paid up. "Adesso (now)?", I asked and he said "Yes", just like Molly Bloom but without the dramatics. I fully expect it all to work out tomorrow but, if not, there will be drama!

Feeling very satisfied with myself, I wandered off to get fed and get beer (not get drunk, I told you I am being good). My phone still would not send a message to Maria so I tried to send one to Anna. After many efforts to activate every function I at last succeeded in sending a message to her and now I really felt I had accomplished much today. So I treated myself to a nice but inexpensive meal at a café that did not wait until 8pm to open. The spicy taste of n'Djou (a local piquant meat or spice, depending on what you are having) went down well, accompanied by 2 "birre grande". When I called for the waiter, he asked was it too piquant, but I told him I loved it and only wanted bread to mop up the sauce left on my plate. I was a very happy man so I called into my favourite bar in Pizzo for another beer and a chat with Franco, his wife Carmen, who also does Sudoku, and Loredana. It went down just as well as the others and then I made my way contentedly to my resting place (not the final one, I hope)

SABATO 7 GIUGNO

"It's four in the morning and once more the dawning has woken the wanting in me!"
At four in the morning I find myself packing to go to my next temporary abode, Mr Plant's mother's house, just up the street. Almost everything fits in the case as it did when I came only a week ago. Birds sing outside and cats squabble and I am not so sure about life at this early hour. I would prefer to be asleep actually.

I pushed myself out of the bed at about 8.30, as I had a lot to do, like getting my internet connected and moving to the apartment I was renting while the house was being completed. I had my usual cappuccino and waited for the phone shop to open when Carmen came at 9.30. She greets me and I explain I got no message from TIM but I had not the TIM Sim card in as I phoned with the Vodaphone one. She put it in and tried to sort it but said I would have to wait for the text message from TIM. I then phoned Mr Plant and arranged to meet him to move out his B&B and into his mother's apartment. This was accomplished fairly easily, apart from having to drag my bags down the many steps and waiting for him to arrive (he is Italian and laid-back about time) and then pulling them up the cobbled street. The apartment is fine and soon I was ensconced and organised and ready to go out again to buy some stuff when I looked out and it was lashing again! So, back to the computer to write this, and hope for better weather. It was ok and his mother had left me a lovely arrangement of fruit, elegantly laid out, as is the norm, it seems, with everything most Italians do! I had some melon and by then the rain had stopped.

So I went back down the piazza, bought some mayonnaise, butter, bread, washing liquid (detergent? Liquid not powder) for the washing machine, and the T-shirt with "SONO PIZZITANO" (I am of Pizzo) enscribed. This I had to show to the Carmen in the bar, if not the one in the phone shop. Franco was too busy in the bar and Carmen thought it "Bella!" and showed me her Sodoku book. I guess we were sharing something. Then it was into the phone shop but the other Carmen told me I would have to wait for the text message from TIM. "Feck TIM" I felt like saying but desisted and was told to come back at 6pm, as it took 24 hours to get the thing activated or something. This is getting on my nerves and I am losing patience. I don't even know if the phone is even working properly, as text messages I sent have not been received, although phone calls have! I also got messages from Vodaphone when I bought their Sim card and phone, but none from TIM since I bought their Sim card, not even limited service messages like I did with Wind!

I take time to forget about it for a while and relax (mustn't get obsessed and paranoid!). I buy an ice cream from my friend in Bar Ercole Gelatario l'Originale, who told me I was a Pizzitano, so I show him the T-shirt and he laughs heartily and tells his friend the story of how he suggested my inscription on the T-shirt. After the ice cream I decide to have lunch and go to the place where I got the panino superbo and the pasta with n'Djou (SPQR). I try something else and it is fine and cheap also. A few men in suits drive and park their cars in the piazza and walk self-importantly, it seems to me, with their well-dressed women into the restaurant next door. When the tourist train/bus comes back it finds itself unable to just turn around as usual in the piazza. The driver walks around looking for the car owners. I indicate to him that they have gone into the restaurant but he comes out without finding them, it seems. He sits up in his cabin and starts to "beep" loudly and long but no response comes and he tries the restaurant again. He waits for about 10 minutes and starts to reverse his machine with difficulty but he manages to turn it around and get back into the centre of the piazza. Because the Festa Fragole (Strawberry Festival) is on, there are tents, a platform and stalls set up which made it even more problematic for him but all ends well, except the car owners never did return to their cars while I was there. I began to wonder were these the untouchables, members of the Camorra, or prominent politicos, who answer to no one? More importantly, would I be in trouble for indicating knowledge of their whereabouts? Interfering in local life might be a problem, I wondered.

Back to my apartment to do my washing I went, but could not get the machine working so I texted and phoned Paolo to get his father down to show me how it worked. I still don't know which worked, the text or the phone, but he came anyway and sorted it out and showed me the bottle of gas and how to turn it on and off for cooking. There are millions of things to learn about living in Italy. I think I am doing quite well, apart from the texting and the internet. I will not give up, however! Music blares out from somewhere and I go to investigate. The local church at the top of the road is celebrating its patron's feast, as well as the Festa Fragole (yes ..the Strawberry Festival). Flags are out and the street is decorated and other preparations are on-going. I head for the music and wander into the church. It is beautiful and has many fine murals or frescoes depicting San Francesco de Paola. I take some photos, especially of the decorated statue of the saint and the murals on walls and ceilings. Somehow, I don't feel threatened or suppressed by this, the Italian form of the religion and its displays.

Later, I wander out to view a football match, check in with Carmen in the phone shop, and take in the Festa Fragole. The first match of the European Championship 2008 starts at 6 pm between Switzerland and the Czech Republic and I am just in time for it. At half time I go to tell Carmen I have received no text from TIM and I am not too pleased to be told I must wait more. I mention to her that she told me it would be in today or at least 24 hours after I bought it. At this stage I am getting annoyed for the first time since I came to Italy and I tell her I am not happy, that I have paid almost €200 and have nothing to show for it.

"It's crazy" I say and then "Non felice" (not happy).
"You must wait" she says.
"How long?" I ask, and she just replies
"This is what they tell me"

When I remind her she told me yesterday it would be ready today and this morning that it would be 24 hours since yesterday, she just repeats her mantra "You must wait" staying calm as she always is, but feeling embarrassed, I think. It's probably not her fault but I am still losing my cool. I manage not to get too excited and try to remain as philosophical as I was earlier this week.

"What's another few days?" I think. "Why am I getting so obsessive about this? Nobody is crying out for my emails etc". I let it go and try the new me. If it doesn't work out in a few days, I will not be so understanding. Italy doesn't always work for me, it seems. Activating gadgets like mobile phones and internet connections takes time. Ireland may be a bit ahead in areas like this, which surprises me, as I had imagined Italy to be very advanced in technology and design. Is administration the problem?

The piazza starts to fill up for the festival and I enjoy the rest of the match, which the Czech Republic won. I decide to eat and have a beer and the second match starts between Portugal and Turkey which I had not known about. Before it starts, I manage to get some of the strawberries, a little wine, and queue for the helpings from the giant strawberry cake. Everybody mills in and there is good-natured chaos. The life in the piazza is amazing. Crowds are watching the match on an outdoor big screen, people are eating and drinking, children are running around while others are sharing a meal with their parents or families at tables. Extra staff have been employed to deal with the crowds and no one seems to be stressed. All this is happening outdoors while we in Ireland are all indoors. The weather just makes such a difference and a different culture is at work. Nobody gets drunk, as far as I can see, and I don't feel the need to order another round each time I finish a drink. In fact, I had one beer all evening and retire quietly after the second match, glad to see the skilful footballers of Portugal get their just desserts with a two goal win, not that Turkey were bad.

DOMENICA 8 GIUGNIO

Not drinking seems to help my sleeping and I got my best sleep since coming to Pizzo. Maybe it was the bed in the apartment or the apartment itself but I slept till 8.30. My mood was still not the best, probably because of the lack of success in getting my internet connectivity. I was also aware of the novelty of living here wearing off. I had finished reading my English books and could not connect to the internet and was finding time on my hands. The challenge of daily living and normality was looming and this is what I knew I had to test myself against. Not having Donna to talk to, English papers nor tv to engage with, my books being already read, and really having little or nothing to do but write and just live everyday life in a foreign country without enough of the language to help me socialise or just interact was what I had questioned myself about for years. Could I hack it?

Suddenly, there was noise outside, booming claps of thunder or a very big gun going off. I went out to investigate and found much activity going on, related to the feast of San Francesco of Paola. The balconies were being hung with pictures of him and posters were being stapled or stuck to doors, walls or railings. People were making their way to the church at the top of the road. I abandoned my writing to feel the pulse of the day and the life going on at the time around me. I had come to experience this and I didn't want to miss anything.

Making my way cautiously to the church, I waited outside for a while to view the scene. Stalls had been set up to sell food and other stuff. Uniformed public servants of the Civile Protezione were gathering and many men were standing around like myself. I have not been an attendee at religious services for years but I wanted to have a look and went into the church, which was already almost full of people. The time was 9.50 am and so I guessed the mass would be at 10.00. The church was wonderfully decorated, as I had seen the day before and there were large images of the saint painted everywhere and in different scenes all around. I could not work out if he was the same St Francis of Assisi we all knew but his name was different. More people crowded in, the women minding children and making a fuss of where they sat and how they behaved. Some teenagers were obviously not interested in sitting with parents but they were sorted out and younger children whom I had seen cavorting around the piazza were being carefully controlled. One woman made to enter my pew, the one at the end of the church, of course. She called her grown–up daughter to go into the next one, then left and changed seats and ordered her husband in beside me before changing it all again. The priest entered at the end of a procession of lay people, many of them I had seen working for the tourist board and officials of the civic powers of various hues. Church and state are still entwined in Italy obviously. There was glorious singing and great attention being paid by the congregation, but after about 10 minutes standing I had had enough and vacated my place, granting it to the husband of the fussy woman who had moved across the nave of the church, and may God help him and what I took to be his daughter.

Later in the piazza, a procession of the congregation from the church led by the priest and the statue of St Francis of Paola, and all the helpers, attired in reds, blues, yellows and so on, and also the town band, came down the hill into the piazza. I tried to take some videos on my camera but I had to stop as I had filled up the image card. These celebrations, first last weekend and now this, seemed to be a regular occurrence but did bring excitement. I don't know how seriously religious it is but it makes life and the town more interesting for tourists and locals anyway. That night on my way home there were more celebrations outside the church, with music and singing, accompanied by a lone, barely-clad young lady cavorting on a stage to the music. It did not seem so religious to me but "different strokes for different folks" and all that. It continued until midnight which didn't help me sleep!

For the rest of the day I took myself off to the piazza and the beach.

On my way to the beach I just had to show off my "Sono Pizzitano" top to the ladies in the Pantheon Bar and got Franco, the husband, to take a photo of myself with his wife, Carmen and Loredana, the other member of staff. Coming out of there, I met Felix, the landlord of a B&B I had stayed in last year. He enjoyed my slogan and pointed me out to his friends. From there it was up the piazza, where someone shouted
"Non credo" (I don't believe it, referring to my slogan).
"E vero!" (It's true") I replied in my brilliantly fluent Italian, and we all had a good laugh.

I just had to call into Gelateria Ercole, whose owner, another Francesco, had suggested the slogan to me. I took a photo of him behind the bar then asked for one with him. He introduced me to his father, and we all got into a photo. He told me he wanted a copy and gave me his email address. Strange looks came my way in the piazza alright but I was happy with my announcement and, indeed, was thinking of a few more slogans for tops and even advertising my English classes in this way
"Sono insegnante Inglese, di Irlanda. Telefono............" Or even just,
"Amo (ti?) Pizzo"

I could start a new business in tops with inscriptions. Better get a hold of myself! I could be starting a new trend here, building up confidence in the town, but also coming to the notice of those who might have other interests, the darker side of Italian life!

I had my third swim of the week, collecting my stones and finding a big lemon in the water. Several teenagers and children were playing with a ball found on the beach. One young girl could not be consoled about something for a long time and kicked up a scene and a lot of sand at her brother, it seemed to me. Screaming crying and working herself up to a right pitch, she stormed around the beach, throwing herself on the sand among other dramatics. One brother could get nowhere with her but eventually a bigger one dived into the water from the pier and swam to her and calmed her down in true loving, big brother way. In no time she was playing ball and swimming with them all. I guess Italians are quite able to do the drama queen. Not that it is only the women, a young boy went crazy later in the piazza at the fuzzball table attacking another young boy and then his father and had to be separated, the father shouting "Basta!" at him several times and other fathers joining in to stop the war. It continued for quite some time and the boy was really upset. It was easy to see how distressed he was but also quite funny for us onlookers. Peace was restored however and the game went on.

Having a beer later on after my swim, I was in the right place to observe more Italian dramatics. A convoy of bikers rode in, lead by what looked a bike but the size of a car, easy rider style, yellow, with three wheels, multiple horns and lamps, flags flying and dripping with leather fringes. An American flag took pride of place and seemingly, from what I could hear, he was called "D'Amerigo" or some such title. The marina had already been busy with traffic and traffic police taking charge, maintaining the flow, but this really upset the applecart. Whistles were sounded shrilly and much arm-waving ensued but the convoy did find parking eventually and got the notice it deserved and obviously craved. Other bikes were almost as impressive, all nearly Harley-Davidsons, some BMW, some wonderfully decorated and customised and one with the passenger side car. It was very plush with a golden mascot of some kind in front. People crowded around to see them and photograph them, putting their children in the saddles. One camera man had a large video camera as for professional purposes and he went from one interesting bike to the other. The bikers dismounted and moved to the left of the marina, greeting and kissing each other on both cheeks. They were not always young men either, some with flowing locks, often grey, and moustaches, all dressed in severe black leather gear, some with girl friends also attired so and even one quad bike had a young child in front, the biker and a female partner bringing up the rear. It was a show!

Not everyone was impressed, I felt, including the owner or manager of the bar I was drinking in and a well-dressed customer who seemed to be complaining to him and to anybody who would listen. A phone call ensued to some authority but the bikers left about 30 minutes later, having caused lots of interest but little trouble. The only trouble I saw was when the female partner of "D'Amerigo" parked her accompanying car awkwardly and left it there and another car was prevented from going. It was all sorted, with the help of a policeman, who had to wait then until the female took leave of her mate, but insisted on parking alongside him, blocking one lane of a two-lane stream of traffic. They were waved on and did leave at last.

When I returned to my temporary abode, I was pleasantly surprised to find I had got a message from TIM and so I tried my internet connection and it worked! Unfortunately, my battery warning light also started flashing so now it don't know if I have other problems. I will just have to go to Carmen in the phone shop and try to sort it with her. I finished off my day by watching the next two matches in the European Championships Finals and having my spaghetti, at the exorbitant price of €3 (joke).

LUNEDI, 9 GIUGNO

Naturally, the first thought that struck on wakening at about 6am was to worry about my pc. Would the battery fail? Where would I get a new one in Italy? Would I ever get the internet sorted and had I ruined my pc by buying this TIM card? I remembered how the man in Vibo had said the Vodaphone internet key was the only way to do it and he couldn't sort it. There was nothing to do but get up and face the day.

I immediately went down to the pc and saw the battery light flashing and my heart sank. However, I turned it on and it worked despite the dire warnings it gave me about my battery not being recognised and the system not being able to charge it. I wrote up yesterday's diary and it was still working so I had some hope. I went down to Carmen in the phone shop and she got my internet key working at last. That really helped and kept me happily busy for several hours

In fact, I spent most of the day on the internet sending emails to my wife and family, checking on emails I had received and so on. I asked my wife to bring more English books as I had finished the ones I had. I had the football to watch so it was not so bad. If she could stay all summer it would be better, I suggested, instead of going home for three weeks in August and asked her to try and change her arrangements in work. I attached a photo of the house I was in, where we would be for at least two weeks until our house was completed. She might want to see it and my washing hanging outside!

MARTEDI 10 GIUGNO

Another eventful day; I went to the travel agency up the town (and it is too far to go again!). I asked about train times from Rome for my wife and the assistant said there was one at 6.45 and I thought it would be good so I tried texting my wife, which is when I discovered I had no credit left! Anyway, she must have got one text at least and I went back to the agency when she said "get it". We did it. Then we discovered it was for 6.45 am! Our Italian and English language problem confused the issue probably but I told the assistant it was no use to me, or to my wife. She wanted me to pay for it as she had confirmed it or wanted me to change to another train but pay a penalty of €20. No way! The next train was at midnight almost and arrived here at 6am, which was also not on, I felt. Things became quite heated and I left, probably leaving her with a problem. So I won't be going back. The train my wife wants to get is at 5.45pm, as far as I know, but she may not get from the airport in time as I said before and if I bought a ticket for it, it would not do for the next train, if she were late. I though it best for her to get her ticket at the station in case she was late, especially considering she would have to collect her luggage and might not make it to the train in time.

I am advertising for students for English lessons. So I am printing flyers and getting help from the tourist office with them and with my Italian wording. We will see what happens. I need to be doing it or having a try, at least. I want to make some money also, but maybe I could use classes to get to know people and for socialising and integrating into the community here. My phone credit runs out quickly and is costing me so using email and skype would help. We are still trying to get skype working properly as either the mike or the webcam are causing problems and we are not sure how it all works anyway. I went to the ATM with my new bank card and it worked, thank god!

There was despair, sarcasm, cynicism and laughter here at the Italian defeat last night. I watched the first half in a local restaurant near Antica Terraza (the apartment I stayed in the first week) with a local crowd, mostly the family of the owner, I believe. I left at half time to go to the piazza where Italian flags were flying and the crowds were noisy and more excited, shouting and slagging. I felt at home somehow. Things could be interesting after this poor performance, for Italy and for the supporters.

I must talk to Paolo (Mr Plant) about the house but maybe I will wait until my wife gets here. I want to get down to the details and practicalities, like getting a bidet. In general, I want Italian touches, simplicity, light, bright colours and also, I wonder could we extend the terrace out over the path in front for more room. It is just an idea I have and probably not on, really.

I do think my Italian is coming on. I am trying it out here, as I have to, although it is not always great.

MERCOLEDI GIUGNO 11

I had a phone call from Alessia in Maria's office yesterday, asking did I want to meet this morning with a design guy to help with furnishings and fittings so we met at 9.30am. We went to the house and he measured rooms etc and we talked about it. I said we would not decide anything until my wife came but I gave him an idea of what we wanted, eg. not so much kitchen appliances, but sofa beds, etc. He had some ideas and will get back to us. We met Paolo too and discussed the work and the need to hurry it up to be ready for July. He says he is working as fast as he can, even on weekends, which is true. I suggested he get more workers but he says he has two more working on another job and cannot take them away as he is contracted there too. We discussed various items; painting outside is included in the agreed project, but not inside, so we will have to pay for it. He had a document in Italian, a quotation for extra work, which Alessia will translate for us and also whatever we said today she will keep an account of it for us to read. If we want air conditioning, Paolo must know by next week. We might be wise to get it piped or make connections for it but not get the contraptions yet. However, it is cool enough inside so we may not need it but I was not sure if we would ever be here in winter and need heat. Natural light is a problem as there are only a few windows, at least downstairs, but I asked could he open more and it is not possible because of centro storico laws, it seems. Likewise, I asked about making a bigger balcony and terrace but, "no". The terrace is big enough, I think. I was just chancing my arm.

Anyway, I will send my wife the translation of Paolo's quotation and our discussion points. I have asked Paolo for a key as he hasn't given it to me yet, as there was no point if I could not sleep there. But I want to show my wife the house on Sunday. He will have it for me soon, he says, in time for Sunday.

I also got good news on tennis. It seems there is a communal one up on Via Nazionale. The girl in the tourist board did not know it before and had told me we would have to travel and pay for a private one. I will check it out.

I was asking Paolo about my wife working or learning in an Italian restaurant or kitchen and he thinks it possible. Then I met Francesco, the one who gave me the slogan for my t-shirt "Sono Pizzitano". He is a very friendly gelateria owner and he invited me to have a drink in another restaurant. It is the one where my wife saw them preparing pastries before. I spoke about her to them and they said it would be ok for her to come on Tuesday next to talk to them, if she really wants to. It's lunchtime now and I am indoors a habit I have been adopting for some time now, writing and getting out of the heat in the mezzogiorno.

I am feeling sleepy now as I got up at 5 am so I will have my siesta. I finish an email to my wife and tell her I am "Loving you and waiting for you, my woman who is coming on Saturday".

JOVEDI 12 GIUGNO

I found tennis courts on Via Nazionale (yes, up the hill, where I have to go too often, it seems). They are public ones, in what is called Villa Communale, a community facility, like we played in before, in Peschiera del Garda. When I asked about playing tennis there, one guy working there said "No", it seemed, and another said "yes" so I picked the former to talk to. I think it may be because it is for the youth but the second guy seemed to see no problem and said it would be cheap also when I asked. It may not be what Donna wants, as she prefers doubles and using tennis to mix, and maybe socialise, but if we meet someone in a tourist village we can try there. They are more expensive, I know, but if we come as friends of residents it will be good. Maybe when we go to Italian classes we will meet some such residents.

I also came across the usual weekly market up there today. So it is on Thursdays obviously and Donna will be interested, I am sure.

These local markets are great and are much better on the continent than what we have in Ireland now. They seem to hold on to local customs better in mainland Europe and we seem to adopt British or American ways much too easily. There is real local produce on sale, such as vegetables, meat, fish, crafts, home-made food products, as well as the usual stalls selling all kinds of tat, cheap clothes, electrical goods, trinkets and other rubbish. I am not very interested but I admire the culture of it. I must admit I avoided the travel agency where the Trenitalia ticket confusion arose, just in case. I didn't want to have a scene or get into more trouble.

Paolo came along with the keys for our house at last. I had gone to the house and his office for them and was glad when he finally dropped them in. He is a real Italian, not very punctual and a great one for "Domani" (tomorrow) but I still like him and trust him to do a good job on the house for me, with some good Italian design and features. I have seen his work in the B&B I stayed in, and liked it. He is married, I believe, but Italian style, if you understand my meaning (I am not sure myself, but he didn't answer me very convincingly when I asked him) and has no children. He is a real Pizzitano and knows everybody and everything that goes on in Pizzo and that is useful.

I went a little bit earlier to the beach today and it was just as well as I only got back before it started to rain quite heavily. Seemingly, it is bad all over Europe and I can see that in the football on tv, where some matches were played on waterlogged pitches. Our neighbours were in France for three weeks, my wife said, and it rained all the time. Here it stopped, but it did curtail the open air tv viewing of the second match, which I nevertheless got to see in the SPQR pub. I will figure out the significance of the name on the internet as well as a very interesting slogan on one of the pictures there, "ROMA ORMA AMOR". I intend to let you know when I find out. The words are all anagrams of Amor or Roma, as I am sure you noticed. Sorry about the teaching style!

Germany managed to lose to a very good performance from Croatia. What is the world coming to? Poland surrendered their one goal lead in the ninety second minute giving away a stupid penalty. Isn't it always stupid to give away a penalty, but anyway, you know what I mean? Austria probably deserved a draw as they had missed several good chances in the first half particularly. Boruch, the Polish goalkeeper had done well to save them, in fact.

I have been putting up lots of flyers for my English classes and some have even stayed up but so far there have been no takers. I am not too worried as it means I can have a holiday and look after Donna as she needs a break. It is not the best time for giving lessons to people here, as this is the tourist season, when most people are busy, if they work at all. Winter would be a better bet, but that is a discussion I have had with Donna already and we are not really that interested in living here all year around. My publicity campaign is only starting and it may take people a while to get to know me and to have a go. It will not be a waste of time as these things often do require patience and different approaches. I will even offer free classes, if needs be, to get known and accepted. A philosophical attitude goes a long way here, I think, and is very Italian.

Having espoused the joys of being philosophical, I now have to admit to panic attack. In saving this diary entry on the computer, I made a mistake and substituted it for my whole diary, a very big file I have been adding to every day since coming here. "What a plonker", as Del Boy would say but it just goes to show it is time to stop when you are tired and that is my excuse. It doesn't help with the problem now, but I decided to leave it for another day. Yes, "Beidh la eile ag an bPaorach", as we say in Irish "the Powers (my family name) shall have another day!" Indeed!

VENERDI 13 GIUGNO

Of course, I woke up at 4.30am with my problem of my lost file on my mind and decided to get up and do something about it instead of worrying. I was able to find quite a lot of emails I had sent to people with various accounts of different days. Some even had 3 days writing. Trying to get help from MsWord and DELL was useless. It may be there was a solution available in their programmes or on the website but I could not find it. Those websites are so confusing, I find, and one can never find exactly what one wants. Emailing my family was another idea and I did it to ask them to send me back whatever I had sent them, in order to put the file back together. It was lucky I kept my original notes of what I wrote in the first few days as I still have them and can rewrite them, which may even improve them. So, all in all, all is not lost. It just felt like that. I compiled a historical photo album of my family of origin some years ago and lost all my work during that time so I know this problem. It is a nightmare for writers and others but an occupational hazard. It may make me feel like a writer to write that, but it may also be a positive, one never knows. I find it helps to think like that. Years ago, I would have beaten myself up about it for days and weeks!

Feeling energised, I also decided to clean the house, especially floors and surfaces, like worktops, shelves, steps and presses. Ants had made an appearance in the apartment and I had to try to eradicate them and the causes of such an event. It was quite easy as jobs like this usually are, once you determine to do them. Doing housework everyday is boring, however; another lesson in life I discovered late on, when I had the time to do it. If I am sounding mature and wise, please forgive me. Smugness is not very attractive.

Next, I had to tackle the problem of my computer battery, which is not now recognised by my system and is not charging, so it will not work unless connected to the mains. Amazingly, in spite of my declaration above, that support sites such as DELL's are not very user-friendly, I seem to have made the proper contact and have been receiving emails on how to sort this problem. This time I was told to download a new BIOS system (don't ask, I don't know what it is but if it works!). I did it and my computer restarted itself, but the orange light still flashes, although the message telling me my system does not recognise the battery, no longer comes up when I start up. Time will tell if it is sorted. It works on mains anyway and this is ok for now.

It was raining when I looked out and that disappointed me, not so much for my sake, but for Donna's, who is hoping to come on a real sunny holiday. Usually, it stops quickly enough and I hope this will be the case today but Franco in the Pantheon Bar says "no". As a few drops fall again I decide to get my haircut, as Donna has often suggested to me to do in Italy. It is quite pleasant but we don't talk much due to the language problem. He takes a bit too much off but does a good job, in the Italian style, he says. Hopefully, I will pass the inspection tomorrow. I feel lighter anyway and another bit of preparation is out of the way! Francesco from Bar Ercole notices it and makes some joke, at my expense, doubtless. But I like him, and even being slagged is an accomplishment, I feel. It may mean I am accepted...........or maybe not!

The rain must have put people off for the beach was empty and stayed that way while I was there. To paraphrase Mr Coward "Mad dogs and Irishmen swim in the (not so hot) afternoon"
It was also a bit wilder, with little waves breaking on the beach, and I enjoyed it all the more for that. Not that it was cold or I was being brave or hardy. In Ireland it would have been a good-enough day on the beach.

Then it was back for the big match, Italy v Romania. We were not sitting outside because being a 6pm kick-off game, it was still bright and the picture on the screen would not have been very clear. We were inside in the small bar, where seats and stools had been set out, It was more intimate and exciting and lent itself to creating the proper lively football atmosphere. I almost felt at home, among real football fans. I felt accepted too, especially by the owner,

Francesco, who might have been under pressure to limit numbers to Italians, even "Pizzitani".

Italy, having lost their first game, were up against it. They played well enough after a slow start but Luca Toni still had no luck, missing early chances. When Romania went forward they were dangerous and could have scored, hitting an upright and Buffon saving Italy before Mutu put Romania ahead to the consternation of the crowd in the stadium and in the crowded bar. The agony and excitement had hardly died down when Italy equalised, the bar crowd rising as one, and the noise to a crescendo. It was not a great goal but a free coming across the goalmouth was knocked in by Panucci. Now, we had a game and Italy took over almost but still could not score, and when Romania got a penalty it seemed the day was lost, but Buffon saved a poor effort from Mutu. Now the swing of emotions continued. Luca Toni was pushed over in the box but got no penalty, to the amazement and outrage of my colleagues and me. He may be a great player, trying hard and causing all sorts of problems for defenders, but he has no speed and Napoleon's dictum about being lucky also came to mind.

" Italia non vinci con Luca Toni" (Italy won't win with Luca Toni)

I opined to a big man in front of me, in my broken Italian and feeling maybe I should keep quiet among these ardent fans in a foreign country, He seemed to understand and yet hr did not take my head off!

The game continued thus, Italy controlling and attacking but without success and Romania playing skilful football and being dangerous at times. Their goalkeeper brought off some wonderful saves and should be the man of the match, I felt. Del Piero was taken off and he did seem to be tiring but got a great applause from my bar fellow. He seems to be held in high regard and does look good but again doesn't seem to score enough now and has lost his speed, not surprisingly as he is older now. Neither the attack nor the defence, surprisingly for Italy, were very good. The midfield excelled this time, especially Pirlo, whom I really admire as a skilful and visionary player. Of course, the defence was missing the great Cannavaro, and it showed. Materrazi was injured or dropped after the first game but he had not done so well anyway. The end result was a draw, which may yet not be the end for Italy, depending on the result in the next match, Holland v France. I was dying to enter the conversation about this but my Italian was not good enough.

Holland won this easily, France being a shadow of their great world cup winning team, apart from Riberi who ran and ran and had no luck. Holland had great teamwork and speed, bringing on Robbyn who ran defenders ragged. Van Nistleroy was a real playmaker and held up ball well and they scored 4 great goals to France's one. France scored and for a time made Holland look only ordinary, but more goals changed that.

It had been a great night of football but I had other interests to consider, and decided to investigate the progress on the house. It was the main item on my agenda, or should have been for these weeks. Having got the keys from Paolo I could have a look anytime and I did in the interval between the matches. I was delighted to see more progress, window lintels having been installed; a wall at the top of the stairs in the main bedroom; more pipes laid, and generally I felt encouraged.

I went back to the bar to see the second game but left after Holland took control and saw the rest of the game in my apartment.

SABATO 14 GIUGNO

My wife is arriving today! There are preparations to be made; food to bought, bed linen to be changed, a taxi to book, tidying up and personal ablutions and enhancement to be done (if such is possible!). I go to the supermarket up on Via Nazionale first and queue to buy fresh prosciutto, taking a number when I discover that this is the system. The Italian obsession about food I admire and I am observing the many choices to be made as regards meat, cheese, and so on. I am aware of the whole delicate relationship between customer and shop staff and though I grow impatient I know I have a lot to learn. However, I have a simple request and go on my way. I walk along the street looking for inspiration as to other necessary purchases. An umbrella and seat for the beach might be a good idea and I look but do not buy as I decide I don't want to carry it all the way downhill and probably I can find them nearer to the beach. I look for them in the piazza but am disappointed. Maybe I should have plumped for the ones I saw when I got the idea first. The piazza is busier at the weekend and I try out another bar/gelateria I have not been to, figuring I should give them all a chance and not insult anybody. Donna texts to say she is in the airport and "a coming". The build-up is on!

Reflecting on my two weeks here on my own, I am quite happy, feeling I got the essentials done. The house is signed for legally and bought, arrangements for where we stay while waiting for it to be finished are made, I have my Italian phone and the internet connection sorted. I have made some necessary decisions as regards the work and put the pressure on to get it finished. Pasquale had measured the rooms and will come up with a plan and suggestions for fitting and furnishing it. The electrical contract to get connected is ready. I myself feel good and am probably in the best physical condition I have been for a long time, due to all the walking, climbing steps up and down to the beach and up to Via Nazionale, swimming, eating well and healthily and not drinking too much. I have relaxed also and found new friends and started the integration process. The worst of the problems are over, I believe. In fact, I feel so good I write a little poem. Here we go,

The azure sky,
Another sunny day.
In Pizzo town,
I live, not die!

Drinking my prosecco,
Writing a little verse,
People-watching in the piazza,
Passes the "mezzogiorno".

I await my good wife,
Who arrives tonight
"La bella donna",
The soul-mate of my life.

or even, to paraphrase the well-known song "Dublin can be Heaven", sung by Noel Purcell, a Dublin actor and singer,

"Pizzo can be heaven,
Cappuccino at eleven,
And a passegiata
Through the piazza"

Apologies to the composer!

My wife was to arrive today but it seems the flight was delayed so she missed the 17.45 train and when I texted her she said she was getting the late night train. I went on the internet and found a train coming from Rome at 20.13 and texted her about it but she had already bought a ticket for a non-stop (at Vibo Pizzo anyway) train to Rosarno, which is further south of Pizzo. Furious texts ensued but it was no use and she will have to go to Rosarno, arrive at 07.00 tomorrow, or thereabouts, and get a train back to Vibo – Pizzo, the poor thing!

Life can be tough and it will have taken her almost 24 hours to travel here, while it took me only 12 hours. This flight to Rome may be more trouble than it is worth. Naples may be rough and the return flights to Dublin don't suit at 11.00 am but this is crazy! I am disappointed and had made many preparations but will just have to bear it. Football kept me entertained before I went to bed and waited for the morning. It will be another lonely night for me and her, a tired Donna in a train for almost 8 hours, and then some. She will definitely need a holiday and some loving, tender care.

While sitting and waiting I hear the Angelus bell, ringing out "The Bells of the Angelus". It is calling me to pray (and I don't) but it is somehow comforting and not intrusive, as I find these things in Ireland. Also, I suppose, "Once a catholic, always a catholic". Pizzo is a happy place for me, I feel, which helps a lot. I'm sure there are depressed and poor people here struggling with life and their problems, but the people I see seem remarkably jovial and contented, although they may not have much of the "Dolce Vita". They seem to have a good temperament and, yes, I am reminded of the similarities between us Irish and Italians. We like to think fancifully of ourselves as the "Italians of the North" but there may actually be some truth in the cliché.

DOMENICA 15 GIUGNO

My wife will arrive today, hopefully, after her long journey, a delayed flight, and train travel confusion. Managing to sleep until 6 am, I have to get up then, as I cannot wait any longer. I desist from texting her and plaguing her with more questions, but I think she may have passed through Pizzo at this stage, even if the train did not stop. When we were in Tropea last year we got the night train to Naples from Tropea so it stopped there, at least. However, she has had enough travel trouble and doesn't need my arguments and thoughts at this time. She asked me to just wait for her here and I will, although I wanted to meet her and get a taxi for her. It is sometimes harder to do nothing and trust the person you love.

So I sit, writing this and trying to distract myself and wait for her. She texts me at 7.45 to say she is getting the train at 8am to return to Pizzo at 8.30 and tells me to have a warm bed ready! I scutter around getting everything ready, preparing a breakfast, making the bed, even ironing the sheets to get them warm! Something tells me that is not what she meant but I am trying everything. I boil the water for tea and get the camera to capture her arriving in a taxi and have a look out from the balcony and suddenly I see her looking around for the apartment number which I texted to her. I take a quick photo and shout to her. She looks around for where my voice comes from and is finding it hard to locate me. At last, she does and I run out to greet her. A lady in a balcony on the opposite side of the street, who had been trying to help her, sees us embrace and kiss. I hug my wife hard and tell her I am glad to see her and ask how she is. She is confused, exhausted and stressed, I can see, and I want to do everything to reassure her and make her feel welcome. She just asks me to hold her more.

We make our way back across the street to where we will live for the next few weeks and she lies down and accepts tea and a light breakfast. She unpacks some stuff she brought for me, books, newspapers, cds and whatever else she considers important. I tell her to take it easy and rest. We talk and let her stretch out on the sofa before going to bed, where we both stay for hours. She needs the rest and I am very happy to have her there with me, her perfume alone enchanting me and I tell her so.

The rest of the day is spent much the same, resting between bouts of walking to the piazza and having prosecco and later a meal. I introduce her to some of the people in Pizzo I have come to know and they are delighted to see her. Carmen, in the Pantheon Bar, who had assisted me in my enquiries about Donna's train going to Rosarno last night, is especially welcoming, giving us a special free snack with our prosecci. Everybody is very nice but Donna is not really up for conversation, especially in Italian, so we do not linger long.

We make our way to the house to view progress. Unfortunately, that was not a good idea. She is shocked and aghast at the state of it. It is too much for her and especially when she is low in mood and tired. She gets upset now and then during the day and later at night, her "Home-bird" feelings and fear of being away surfacing as well as the shock of the house in its present state of disrepair and rebuilding. This allied to her problems of being out of her comfort zone, away from home, is now a major disaster for her. I am aware of it and of her problems in this regard generally. As I said before, she did not travel much before I met her and every so often she gets attacks of the "heeby-jeebies". Hopefully, all will be well tomorrow or in a few days. I remember Pescara and us coming home after a week. But we decided all this over the last year, the weather is fine here (unlike Pescara where it rained and the resort was empty) and we have a house to get ready. We are trying out a new life for ourselves and there are bound to be changes and difficulties involved, emotionally as well as physically and practically. I must remain strong in myself but very understanding and aware of her feelings.

LUNEDI 16 GIUGNO

Now the trouble really starts. Donna has a panic attack in the night, wants to back out of the whole deal and go home. She is crying and in real distress. I try to calm her down and get her to take deep breaths. I ask about our relationship and she says it may be over, as she felt she did fine, for the two weeks I was away! Eventually she goes back to sleep and so do I, but this is serious and I find it very difficult to cope with. Having problems with the house and decisions to be made is bad enough, but if the whole relationship is coming apart I see little point in the house. If this is so, things have to be dealt with. Donna feels she is now in such a state that she cannot deal with the house or me and so I am left with a huge dilemma and no idea of what to do and no cooperation from her. She stays in bed all day and says she cannot even get up. I am worried about her health now as well and afraid to leave her, which only puts more pressure on me and her.

However, I have one important job to do today which cannot wait. I must send a signed letter to Dublin by courier and I don't know where to get this service. Making enquiries in the tourist office and elsewhere proves useless. I phone Alessia and she helps and tells me I will have to go to Lamezia. I set off to get a bus or train. I walk out of Pizzo to the train station in the heat of the midday sun. A train is supposed to come at 12.26 according to the timetable on the wall but it does not and the next is at 13.27. I wait for it, almost 90 minutes from the time I arrived in the station. It only goes to a station, Lamezia Terme Centrale, and I have to go to the actual town of Lamezia. So I change trains and go to Lamezia Nicostro and arrive just at lunch time when shops and offices close. Alessia has given me the address but I have to find its location. A visit to an internet café helps and I am directed to the correct street but cannot find the office. Phone calls to Alessia again help and I am told the internet point on the street is the office I need, even though I asked there and the assistant did not know about it! His manager eventually arrives an hour later, as Alessia had phoned him and explained the situation. He does the business and I even phone Alessia half way through to be assured he know what I want and put him on to her on my phone, to check all will be done safely, fast, and that it is the right way to do it.

I get my two trains back and text Donna to ask her to meet me but she says she cannot get out of bed. Exhausted by all the walking and travel, the heat and the stress I arrive back about 6 hours later and find her still in bed and unable, or unwilling, to move or discuss matters. I get some food, having invited her to accompany me and being refused and settle down to watch the match, going to bed straight away after, in silence, hoping she will calm down if I leave her alone. I did for 6 hours and it did not help but I don't know what else to do and don't want to put more stress on her and myself. Sleep comes eventually.

I have been so absorbed by my worries and getting the courier service I have completely forgotten my mother's anniversary. She is 40 years dead today!

MARTEDI 17 GIUGNO

Another night of panic, and this time of silence, as I don't know what to do and so do nothing. When I get up I try to discuss the situation, saying there are decisions to be made, even though I know she is not able for this, but I have to know whether to go on with the house project or not. I tell her she can ring Maria and tell her she is not satisfied with the house progress and if Paolo wishes to back out of the deal we will take our money and do so, but I am not prepared to lose our money as well, on the house. We will already be losing out as a result of paying fees and will have to pay more. I tell her I don't want to do this but the house was purchased on the basis that we would live in it, in Pizzo, for long periods together during the summer at least and if Donna cannot do that, or doesn't want to, as seems now, there is no point. She decides she wants to talk to Maria about that but Maria is in London and we don't know when she will be back. She also wants me to email Maria about this as she is unsure what to say exactly. I am writing an email to Alessia about the works and changes but do not really want to. I feel she must do it herself if that is what she wants. A row breaks out as we go back and forth over these matters and she says she just cannot deal with it all and just wants to go home. I demand honesty about our relationship and the house and that she take responsibility for her decisions and their consequences and cannot keep changing her mind.

Eventually, we decide she is going home and I am continuing with the house project, although nothing is really clear about that. I go to the Commune, the local authority, to arrange connection to water supply and to register the house for postal deliveries. I pass by the house where Paolo greets me and invites me in. He asks after Donna and I tell him she is angry with him for not having the house ready. Although there is more to it than that, I decide not to say more and he shrugs and his father, who is also there, says something about "Donne!" (women). Paolo points out certain developments, like an extra window which he can open in the wall (it was a recess and I had asked could they not be made into windows as it looked as if they were windows once). We discuss other practical matters but I am not really interested then as my anxiety about the whole project and my wife rises to mind. I go on to the Commune, telling him what I am doing. When I get there I am told Paolo must do this business about the water and post, after eventually getting to meet the official involved, who just speaks Italian, but she did phone Paolon and it seems it will be dealt with. Unsure if I got that right, I go, anyway.

On my way to the piazza, I get a text from Donna asking me to let her "go". I reply that I am doing just that and when I ask her to do something for me, like coming to the piazza to talk, she replies that she will wait for me as she cannot get the internet connected to book a flight. I finish my cappuccino and rush back. I get the internet going and she goes on it to book the flight. In silence we sit, she seems to be working away at it and I am reading. Then she says "Ok, I will stay". I am delighted and tell her and we just rest a while there and hold each other.

We got out to the beach later in afternoon and I have a swim and she seems fine but I am still anxious about her, fretting if she is really ok and knowing I will never really know. We stay a while and she goes for a walk in the water and talks to some boys, asking them to help her up the rocky path but they decline for some reason. Maybe their mothers told them not to talk to strange women, I joke when she returns. We go to a café, where I have gelato (ice cream) and she has cappuccino. She wants to find out about activities in the area, like water sports and tells me she does not want to be isolated. Later we go to the tourist office and ask about facilities and train and bus timetables. When we come back to the apartment we call "home", for the present, it seems things are better and we plan to go out for dinner and to watch the big match. Italy are playing France, both of whom need to win to stay in the competition if Holland beat Romania, as seems likely, and go through as group winners. The meal is fine and we sit and enjoy the match, but had not reserved seats and have to take a back seat this time. All seems fine and we finish watching the match at "home" as Italy are winning 2-0 and seem assured of a place in the next round, Holland also winning.

Sleep comes quickly, after I go on skype and the internet for a while, and all seems much better as we finish the day and I tell my wife I am delighted she is with me.

MERCOLEDI 18 GIUGNO

Today was a great day. Donna and I worked out our attitude to the house and she began to relax and enjoy herself. We are going ahead with the house and Donna is leaving it to me mostly, as she is a bit stressed and feels she cannot deal with it in her present conditions. This is fine by me and leaves me free to get on with it and also I know she is going to be alright, which releases me from my fear and strengthens my position in dealing with everything. Her homesickness has not gone completely but she has decided to fight it and stay with me.

In the morning we went to the supermarket and looked for a beach chair and electrical adaptors as well as checking out the tennis courts I had discovered last week. Nobody seemed to know how to deal with us there, and there was no official or office, but the gate was not locked so we could have played and probably would at some stage.
We went to the beach and had a grand time. First of all we discovered a small beach nearer to us, called Seggiola, used by boats and fishermen, by walking around from our usual beach along the cliffs. It was great to find some local authentic "colour" and real lives, hardworking men, fixing nets and boats, and other "Pizzitani"; women and children swimming, relaxing and generally "living". We saw ducks and ducklings and a little drama. A man threw a scrawny duckling in with the duck and her little yellow chicks, who were paddling along between the boats and tried to get it accepted, it seemed. Where it had come from I do not know.

However, it was pecked and picked on by the other ducklings and even the duck itself and did not get a warm welcome, but plenty of bullying and aggression. Eventually it swam away and had to be rescued by another man. Maybe it was the runt of the litter or an orphan duckling, but nature was not kind to it, nor was the intended adoption family. Real nature is not always the beautiful concept advertising tries to sell us, or which some people have illusions about.

I had a swim and later we had a few drinks in a nearby bar. It was later than usual for us to be in the marina and places were opening and getting ready for customers, which we had not seen before. There was new life there and my wife enjoys that time of day best and it was great to see her have a good time, drinking prosecci.

A girl working in the bar was interested in learning English, she told me, but as she worked all the time for the summer she did not have time for classes. So I started teaching her there and then with little phrases, which I also wrote down for her. They were too simple as she informed me and I asked her what exactly she wanted. "Conversational English" was what she required, so I wrote out the usual questions one learns and uses at the beginning and gave sample answers and told her I would be back the next day to see if she understood and had learnt. She was quite glad I believe, and asked about my fees, which I told her, but I also said it would be free what I was doing then, as it was so short and she was working and had little time. Maybe she was also conscious of her boss who might say she was wasting time. He seemed nice enough and made no comment. Her name was Aurora and she seemed very pleasant and interested. She also explained someone had taken my flyer so I gave her a new one to put up.

Later, instead of eating out, we bought a take-away pizza from a local restaurant and just read and relaxed in our apartment, as well as going on the internet and Skype. It had been our best day together since my wife arrived. Maybe everything was going to be alright!

JOVEDI 19 GIUGNO

I had my best sleep for a long time and Donna had a better one too, not having any panic attack during the night, but not altogether free from negative feelings. It was great to start a day in better shape and we were soon off to the weekly market up on Via Nazionale. It was a disappointment to me really but it brings lot of colour, excitement and people too, into the life of the town. We did not find adaptors or beach chairs and even Donna could not get interested in buying any of the trinkets or cheap clothes and stuff. We then toddled off to another supermarket and did not got them there either. Later we had coffee, a beer and prosecco at a nearby café where we took a photo of the autostrada bridge, which was so near the town and talked about renting a car maybe for the visit of our family. We just relaxed there for a while and took our time and I was glad to see my wife do just that. We did get two cheap beach chairs (the last of the line and cheaper than we saw them elsewhere but the shopkeeper would not allow further haggling over the price, just because we got 2) and some fruit and roast chicken. Before returning to our apartment we called into the local church, which my wife wanted to see, and which is beautiful, with huge paintings and murals of San Francesco of Paola, stain glass windows, light streaming in from the roof and an air of calm, which she just soaks up. She checked out all the notices and says she wants to join the choir and go to mass there. Then we called into the office of Calabrian Invest, a property company from England, but which also advertises outside that it publishes an English newsletter for Pizzo, and three lovely ladies welcome us in and we talk about various ideas as to how to socialise and how we might contribute to the newsletter, which I offer to subscribe to. They are still seeking permission to distribute it monthly and so for now it is only available on the internet. I am able to tell them of a school for learning Italian they did not know about, which we have enrolled in for a week. We swap email addresses and promise to keep in touch, maybe even at the school. Donna is happier now as she feels she needs someone to talk to in English as well as trying her Italian. Things are definitely looking up. There is also an exhibition, which we go into, of San Francesco art objects, mostly wooden carvings and sculptures that entrance Deirdre, in a small building near the church. After that we had a very nice lunch in our apartment with our purchases.

The internet kept us busy for about two and half hours then, each of us checking and writing emails. Alessia sent me a list of new costs, some optional, some not, from Paolo and his latest time scale for completion of the house, the end of July! I reply and tell her I need to speak to Maria and Alessio as soon as possible and that I am very angry at this and Paolo's increasing costs, such as for windows, which surely were included in the original price.

We descend to the fishermen's bay in the afternoon where another drama is enfolding. There are naval policemen, a diver, and a "Civile Protezione" vessel in the cove and a local shouting at them. They seem to be looking for something but only find old tangled nets and an old chair. The fishermen put a boat in the water and off some of them go, the rest retreating to steps to observe the search. Is it a drugs search or what? We do not know. Photographs are taken of the vessel and its find by the policeman. I take some photos of the policeman, the vessel, the fishermen and their boats, and the ducks and ducklings we saw the day before. There is no sign of the scrawny one. We hope to find out the story of the search sometime.

This evening we get a little dressed up, a la passegiata, Italian style, and go to the marina a little later, to see the yacht exhibition. We never find it but I never did believe a flotilla might arrive but there was a notice about something to that effect. My English student has done her homework in a little notebook and I correct it. It is almost perfect except for a misuse of the future and the conditional. We talk and I write some grammar points on the same and give her some more conversational English in writing as well as verbally. Donna phones Anna, our daughter, who is returning today from a holiday in Portugal, and also expecting the results of her degree exams. She has passed all the tests and will not have to repeat, which is great as she is to come to us for a week and would have missed that if she had to repeat. She is a little disappointed with her results, having expected more A's or such and we try to cheer her up and tell her we are very proud of her. We have a few drinks and sit on a bench at the marina. There is a big screen at one end and I ask if the football will be shown on it and get two different answers, the owner (I think) asking me to come back later and he will sort it out. As there is little action we just walk up the steps, have an ice cream and prosecco in Bar Ercole, and I introduce my wife to Ercole. We toddle off to SPQR to see Germany defeat Portugal then, in a great match. I see a potential student I had spoken to previously and talk to him about tennis, and we try to arrange a game for the morrow. He is interrupted by a call and disappears. I hope we haven't scared him off.

VENERDI 20 GIUGNO

There are no calls from Maria about the house or from Francesco concerning tennis. We go around the corner, near the church of San Francesco of Paola, to get the bus to Vibo to look for adaptors. Donna has not been there and we have been told it is good for shopping.

It is an overcast day so the views are not so astounding but good enough still. We get off and start to find our way. First stop is a beautiful café where we have cappucini and some delicious free snacks. Next, to the phone shop where I bought my Italian phone, and I get some phone credit. Asking about adaptors, we are given helpful directions, plus a roughly drawn map, to a shop specialising in same. We find the street alright but it is right at the top of it and we have to a buy a whole pack of adaptors to get what we want. I have mentioned sandals so I am brought in and have them bought for me. It will be nice to get out of tennis shoes. We then try to find a tourist office and did notice a sign for it but cannot remember where. We go all the way back to the phone shop to be told we have to go up another street. This street would have been a much quicker way to the adaptor shop, we realise, and we actually find a shop on it which sells a universal adaptor and it is less than half the price of the packet we got. The tourist office is up there also and we are just in time before it closes for lunch. We get some information but none about water sports or bus timetables, which we wanted. Back down the street again to have lunch, where I had it in my previous visit to Vibo, the week before. It does not disappoint, Donna relenting and having most of my fish lasagne. The tickets we have will not do on this bus, which belongs to a different company but we care not and lash out our €2 extravagantly.

Siesta is called for and we follow. I sleep for about two hours and then it is off to the beach at the marina. We bring our chair and umbrella and the sun comes out, the best part of the day. My student is not working in the café where we have ice cream but turns up later saying she hasn't had time to study. "Domani" we agree. It is Donna's favourite time of day and we relax in the evening sun. We meet Paolo and it is a bit awkward but I see little point in talking to him, as I don't understand what he says, and I want to let him know I am annoyed at the delays and extras costs. However, he is pleasant enough and a row will not solve the problem. We buy our milk, water and prosciutto crudo and go back to have a simple dinner with salad, cold hard-boiled eggs and our other ingredients and it is satisfying and sufficient. I watch the match, which is boring enough, but eventually goes to extra time, when both teams, Croatia and Turkey score in the last two minutes and penalties decide it in favour of Turkey! We go on the internet and check our emails and retire to bed happily.

SABATO 21 GIUGNO

Just like Maeve Binchy says in her book, if you want to be a writer you have to write and make time for it, no matter what. So I do. Waking at about 5 am, I write my diary for yesterday and rewrite some other days' accounts which I had somehow lost. However, I had handwritten notes. Now that my wife is here, I find it hard to cut myself off and write, so this time in the early morning is the best maybe.

Later, I go back to bed and we both don't wake until 11am. We must have been tired. I am more than happy my wife is able to sleep peacefully and relax, after her problems earlier in the week. It is off to the supermarket then with my trolley, the wheelie laptop bag my children had given me on the night of my 60th. Birthday party (the laptop followed, once I had decided on it). Both bag and laptop are now coming into their own. We call into a greengrocers and the panficcio (bread baker) before making for the macelleria (butcher) lady with the roast chickens. She is very excited to see us, explaining we were on tv and even going to the trouble of getting a man next door who speaks English, to tell us. We are "famosa"! It is because we were on the beach at the cove used by the fishermen when the local policemen were searching for something a few days before. We ask him "Perche? (why were they searching. and for what?) but he does not know, he says. Maybe a little "omerta" (silence in matters of the mafia) apt.

The chicken is our lunch, along with salad ingredients, and then we go into our emails and take it easy until it is time for our daily swim. We are settling into a nice routine. Back we go to the cove with the ducks and the boats and there are more divers around than usual. Are they looking for what was missed by the naval police? One guy has a bag strapped to him when he gets out and I ask him what he has. "Bananas of the sea" he tells me and they do look like some aquatic fruits. I write some postcards for my sisters and brothers, all along the same theme

" The sun is warm, the sky is clear, the waves are dancing…" (Shelley's lines)

"and we are here!"……………

" but the house is still not finished."

And there is still no call from Maria or Alessio.

Walking back up the steep incline is not easy but good for our "chiselled calves", which is my wife's latest mission and slogan. We upload recent photos on to my wife's Bebo site, not without difficulty. I suggest we go to look at the house. Work is progressing, alright. The terrace wall has been capped, the wall at the stairs and a doorway has been erected on the first floor and a final layer of plaster is in place in many rooms. I show Donna the recess where a new window can be opened. Another similar possibility for a window is above the area for the "Angola cottura" (a small cooking/kitchen corner). She says we will need bright warm colours for much of the inside and suggests a shade of yellow for the outside walls, as well as making notes of other matters needing attention. The side door is no more, it seems, as a window ledge has been erected there, which surprises us, but as it is to be a toilet and shower room inside it, this makes some sense maybe. We just feel we need to talk to Paolo about many details and wish our agents would ring to arrange a discussion. We make a list of items to discuss. I resolve to call them myself and my wife says to leave it until Monday morning if they have not contacted us at the weekend. It is good to see the work is progressing but it will still be some time before it is finished. Our attitude is positive, however, and we are going to see this through.

Then it is time to get ready for the music and entertainment at the marina, which we have seen advertised on posters. "What to wear?" is my wife's cry, amazingly. It is a regular enough cry, but the way these Italians dress up for a simple walk would leave one to believe some care should be taken for a bigger event such as this. It is really no problem for my beautiful, glamorous wife but she still must decide and be happy with her choice. I try a bit myself and tell her she looks gorgeous, which she does. While I wait, I try to do some work on photos and have to recharge the camera battery. All this technology takes time and effort and I seem to be doing a lot of it lately. Skype, internet connectivity with new devices, new phones and the digital frame have kept me busy. It is great when it works and my wife is really taking to it, especially skype and emails and I think it helps to settle and reassure her that she can contact our children and her family and friends. I use the computer mostly for writing, which keeps me right too.

At about 8pm we make our way to the piazza and stop there for a while, as we are too usually too early for events, and there is a good buzz around. Some stalls have been set up at the far end of the piazza and Donna buys a ring and we sit to have a prosecco. Francesco from Bar Ercole greets us warmly, telling my wife she looks “bella”. It is Saturday night and we are all dressed up and have somewhere to go. Anticipation is a great man!

When we walk down to the marina it looks lively enough but soon it is even more crowded and the music starts. It seems there will be some sort of talent competition and my wife is hoping for a dance, but Aurora, my English student (who tells me she will have her English done by Monday) does not know if this will happen. Beer and prosecci follow and we clap and acclaim the singers loudly. Others don’t seem to bother. One big man sings a lively tune and we award him our top marks. There is a huge crowd now. The restaurants are “jammers” and I try to get a table and am told to come back in half an hour. I would like a nice sit-down meal but my wife is not fussed and eventually I just get a take-away pizza. We eat it at our table outside the bar/gelateria, first checking with Aurora that it is acceptable. Donna is almost dancing in her seat and I know it will be a problem until we get at least one dance but everybody else is so laid back it is unbelievable. The singers are getting little attention and certainly nobody is dancing. I check out the Holland v Russia match and am amazed when I discover Russia are winning one nil. We move bars and have an ice cream and, of course, we get up to dance. It is grand and Donna is having a good time. We draw interested glances from people but we don't care and they don't seem to mind, even enjoying it and smiling at us. We both check out the match and now it is a draw and extra time. Then Russia gets two goals to finish it off in style. Having had our dance, we are happy enough to leave it at that and climb up those many steps to the piazza where I have another drink. Donna seems happy to linger and I am happy to oblige. She says she enjoyed it all when we get back to our apartment and is glad she stayed. What a change from the start of the week! It is great for me too and I tell her I am so glad she did.

DOMENICA 22 GIUGNO

It is now three weeks since I arrived in Pizzo and a week since my wife arrived. We have got into a certain daily routine of going out in the morning, returning at lunch time, going for a swim and then eating out or in, watching the football or strolling in the piazza, and me having an ice cream or a drink before retiring for the night. This is a stage we are at, while waiting for our house to be completed, the details and practicalities of which we must also deal with, as when decisions have to be made and official duties or meetings require our attention.

Things will change when we get the house and try to get it furnished and fitted out, especially in preparation for the visit of our children, Anna and Mark, and Anna's boyfriend Liam, who are all due in August. Later Bernard, our second eldest and his partner Olive will arrive with their new daughter, Anna Marie. We are looking forward to it but also worried everything will not be ready and Donna is trying to find suitable activities to keep them entertained, like water sports which do not seem to be available in Pizzo, according to the tourist office staff and others. They will be fine, I tell her.

So as regards this diary in future, there is little need to concentrate on the quotidian which I have been describing for the past three weeks. Instead the house and its concerns, events, and reflections on all that this new life offers and entails will be the topics I will concern myself with usually. I hope I have not bored you to date and expect you now know the daily routine and do not need it repeated ad nauseam. The pleasant nature of this life and my new lifestyle will be the backdrop to whatever happens. The peaceful, simple life I have enjoyed here thus far is what I am aiming for, maybe in slightly different circumstances, as, for instance, when we have our own house. Life throws up a lot of the unexpected and we will deal with it, as best we can. Simplicity is usually deceptively difficult, however.

Today my wife went to mass in the beautiful local church of San Francesco of Paola, and found herself at a First Holy Communion Ceremony. The first few pews in the church were empty but decorated with flowers when she went in and she thought it might be a wedding. There was much shuffling around in the other pews with men being ordered up to the front by womenfolk and declining, very reminiscent of Ireland and Kilbride, County Meath, a country area outside Dublin where we had lived for 17 years, and where our children had gone to primary school, and made their first holy communions. She came out to see the bride and could not, and almost found herself without a seat, when the twenty or so first communicants turned up along with their beautifully turned out, fussing parents.

I had gone back to sleep after getting up early to write. When she came in she was in great form and had enjoyed the mass and now wanted to go for a cappuccino. This was done and she decided to buy some pastries or "dolci" in a shop near the piazza, where the owners engaged her in conversation and explained I was to be a "cavaliero", a gentleman or her knight, by carrying her dolci, while she got the two little tokens of sweets they gave her. She was "flying". Meeting Felix, in whose B&B we had stayed last year, she informed him we were going to go to Italian lessons and he said we could do it much more cheaply by employing a local laureato (graduate) who lived near our new house. He also invited her to learn Italian cooking from his mother-in-law, who was a very good cook, when she mentioned that. She said she wanted to learn these things but also to go to class to meet people and make contacts, which he understood. Of course, he had to tell me I was a very lucky man, my wife being so beautiful. I'll have to watch Felix!

Mass had definitely gone to her head or energised her, for she then wanted to go on the new tourist train. It was full by the time we asked and we were told "Dopo" (later). Well, it turned out to be "dopo" alright, as it seemed to take forever to return and she was just about to go back to our apartment to put the dolci in the fridge, the sunshine being so strong it was almost melting them, when it finally reappeared. Off we went to the "Chiesa di Piedigrotta"(church/grotto), one of the famous tourist sights of Pizzo, about a kilometre or three outside the town towards Marinella. There is a church/grotto there (it was once a cave) and statues and pictures are carved out of the tufo, the local soft rock, which is everywhere. It is famous for being so easily sculpted and is a great construction resource. This stone, local to Calabria and Puglia in Southern Italy, had featured in one of those "Your Place in the Sun" programmes we had seen on tv, when a couple of artists/sculptors were using it for their house and art. The grotto was impressive, as were the steps and the walk down to it (about which I complained, of course), and the whole place is quite dark, and is being conserved, renovated, and developed, as a very important site and tourist venue. The bus/train took us back to Pizzo, to the marina, and out towards the train station, before returning to the piazza………… a grand ride and well worth the fee, with a very enthusiastic driver and music to boot!

The beach was more crowded, even when we came later, bearing our 2 beach chairs (which will be useful in our new house also), our umbrella and our bags. Stalls had been set up at the far end of the marina, it being a Sunday and a day for families on the beach.

The big match was on, Italy v France, and we dressed for the occasion and had booked our seats this time in the piazza, at the open air tv screen of the SPQR bar. There were lots of regulars and two engaged us in conversation, asking had we bought a house in Pizzo. Sandro and Sara, a married couple, were very nice. He had been a sailor, knew some English and had been born in a one-room apartment, where his parents and seven siblings lived, on the street where our house was to be, in Via Campanella. He offered to cook for us anytime, when my wife invited him to visit. He also had a relation married to a girl from Southampton who could translate for us if required. Networking is great and my wife is very good at it, especially today. Sara was interested in Irish writers and knew of Joyce when I mentioned him. U2 were on the telly (on a different station) before the match singing "Still haven't found what I'm looking for" and made us proud to be Irish.

The match was tense and scoreless for the 90 minutes and extra time and went to penalties. The staff were kept very busy, getting drinks and food for the excited multitude of spectators. I ordered two beers when I got my chance, in case I would be left waiting and thirsty, typically Irish. Locals were interested in us and nodded, and were informed by Sara and Sandro about us. Seats were shifted as a people strained to see through the crowd. Gate-crashers who had not booked got themselves into trouble, but all in a good-natured way. Italy were still missing their great Cannavaro, captain of the world cup winning team and Pirlo also, their best player, in my opinion, was not playing, probably because he had got 2 yellow cards in the matches before this. It showed. Italy were not so great at controlling the midfield and the vision and guile needed to open the Spanish defence was lacking. Luca Toni was playing and he just reinforced my view of him, missing chances, being too slow and cumbersome, while working hard and causing some panic in the opposition goalmouth. De Rossi played well in a defensive position and almost made up for the loss of Cannavaro. Penalties decided it and Italy missed two and although Buffon saved a Spanish effort, when Fabregas scored the fourth goal, it was all over! The crowds quickly scattered, disappointed and beaten, but there were no great recriminations. Anyway it had been a great evening and I was glad I had been a part of it. I am a different man in Pizzo maybe, more relaxed.

There are still 3 matches left, two semi-finals and the final, and I will enjoy them for the football, pure or not, and not feel some team has to win and so not get the gut-wrenching feeling I do with Ireland or here in Pizzo, with Italy. Francesco, the SPQR manager or maybe owner, will not do as well out of the games when Italy are not involved and I shook his hand afterwards to thank him and commiserate with him. He was wrecked. He works hard and deserves the rewards for his enterprise.

LUNEDI 23 GIUGNO

The house was in my thoughts immediately I woke up. I made my case about it to myself and printed pages of emails and plans so as to prepare for my telephone call from Maria. She had been in London and had got back on Thursday and was supposed to call me over the weekend and hadn't, and I was now going to call her but I wanted to be prepared and have my facts and story ready. When I did call, she said she had just been about to call me, of course. She said she could not meet me as soon as I wanted. Wednesday was the earliest, but that Alessia was in Pizzo that morning and could meet me, if that would help. I agreed to this as there were matters she could clear up and I needed to talk anyway. Maria said she would get back to me to arrange it but as Donna and I walked down to the piazza (the phone signal is not good where we lived at the time) we met Alessia who was looking for our house, she said, and had forgotten where it was. I almost walked past her but she stopped me, and was introduced to Donna and we got down to business straight away.

We went to the house and I immediately launched into my list of questions and efforts to clarify the situation. The back door had been removed and a window seemed to be going in its place and we had not been consulted on this. The terrace wall could not be removed, and a railing installed instead, as it was a supporting wall, Paolo had told her. I said I did not really believe this and she understood my sentiments. We viewed the house and I pointed out another recess I thought could be a window and she said she would bring all these matters to the attention of Maria and Paolo. I made strong representations that Alessio should be involved as he was an architect and could argue our points as an equal with Paolo. She agreed but said she did not know of his whereabouts. She said it was a difficult working situation for her, with Maria and Alessio splitting up, but she did not really want to talk about it. We went for a coffee and, as she had to hurry to meet clients, we made our points as best we could and she promised to inform Maria and get back to us. As before, she seemed to understand our situation very well and to be empathic about it. I felt she was on our side and she admitted she would be equally angry and unhappy in our situation. She does a good job and I trust her. When we returned to our apartment, I made a synopsis of what had been said and clarified it with Alessia, and sent it to her later. It neatly encapsulates the issues and my attitude at the time so it might be useful to read it here

"Following our short conversation this morning I just want to clarify:

1. **We need more urgency about finishing the house...there is no more important point than this… I have suggested several ways..one way is more workers.. another is to finish one floor as a matter of urgency..any other ideas I am open to…a more detailed time scale might be a good idea..eg. when will floors be done?..electrical connections and water etc?..tiles and painting inside and out (painting outside: maybe when house is finished and we have moved in)?**
2. We don't need air conditioning now, we feel……… so the walls need not be opened again and the "tubes" already installed will

do if we ever want to add radiators, etc…**don't let this delay us any further**

3. the recess window over the Angola cottura.. possible to open up a window there?
4. the new window over the stairs is already agreed and is this what is referred to in extra costs?.. if 2 new windows can be opened we will pay, once it is reasonable
5. **the door at the back and to the side on the ground floor is gone** and we were not consulted and would like to know why.. if possible we would like to have it…….. as otherwise the space outside is wasted and a second door on the ground floor would be good.. the details of his plan for that area we don't know and would like to be informed of. I am sending as an attachment the original plan ..which still includes the door and a WC. We need to be consulted on this area and all other details…hence the need for a meeting and to involve Alessio
6. Inner doors should be white or bright, at least………are the original doors to be used or replaced? We need to be told the details on this and to be consulted
7. accommodation issues during the delay need to be addressed..as I said before we are not willing to pay more when we are the ones being delayed
8. Mr Plant to arrange postal and water registration and connections with the council
9. bidet in shower room /WC/toilet upstairs
10. arch as in original plan and at no extra cost.. painted wall finish? (is that it?)
11. ..is the floor of the terrace to be raised more than at present?
12. Alessio to be involved and another report on the work done since the last one to be given to us

If possible, confirm this (our understanding of the situation) and give answers where needed or comment on these points

Thank you for meeting us Alessia and I will be raising these issues, and more probably, with Maria and Alessio. I think you know our strong feelings about these matters and especially the delay and you have conveyed them to Alessio and Maria.."

We stayed on having capuccini when she left and Carmen in the Pantheon Bar chatted to us. She is really very nice. Frank, her husband, had won €50 on a lottery scratch card and I encouraged Donna to have a go as she often likes to do that in Ireland. Carmen bought it for her, disclaiming all responsibility. Donna won €10 so she bought another one and kept €5, the original cost of the card. That was the extent of the winnings!

During our usual visit to the beach, I met Leon, Lorraine and some friends of theirs from Calabrian Invest, when I went to talk to Anna, my student in the gelateria, who was not in. So I just left my next lesson with her boyfriend, who works there. Leon and I agreed to get together for a drink and he was interested in my idea of forming a group of English speakers, locals as well as English and Irish. Leon looks a bit like "El Tel", Terry Venables, who had been in the running for the Irish soccer manager's job recently.

On the way back through the piazza we met the driver of the tourist bus/train who called Donna over and offered to take us up and down to the beach in future, a very kind offer. We must have looked wrecked and bedraggled altogether after our walk up the many steps from the beach. He introduced us also to Matteo who had been master of ceremonies at the music the other night on the marina and he had also been singing a lot. We complimented him on his performance and were glad to have met another local, one who obviously got involved in community activities, a trait I like. Donna had also helped a man at the beach who was cleaning plastic and other rubbish from the water and beach. He had said nothing, maybe having no English, but I liked the way people took responsibility in Pizzo for the environment and many seems to work for the good of the area and tourism also.

We played our first tennis here tonight. Luckily, we met Francesco, a potential student of English, who had been introduced to me by Frank of the Pantheon Bar. He drove us to the tennis courts and got a friend, who had a key, to get us in. We had been told it was always open but it was locked, in fact. Otherwise we would not have been able to play. They watched us for a while. Donna won the first four games and I was lucky to eventually draw 6 all with her. We left it at that as we had to go to the supermarket and, anyway, I was very tired from all the walking and playing tennis on a hard court. Donna's glasses were not the best for tennis and she was having difficulty with the fading light. My knees were giving me grief and we sat and had a beer before walking down the hill again. It was early to bed for me but I could not sleep for some time. Relief came eventually.

MARTEDI 24 GIUGNO

We had talked of going to Reggio Calabria today, but I could not find train times as the Trenitalia website said the station did not exist! This has happened before and seems to be a regular problem with Trenitalia. When checking my emails I was surprised to find one from Alessia, saying Maria would meet us today, after all, and would phone to make an appointment. Alessia must have convinced her of our serious problems with the house and Maria had decided to see us and it for herself. The phone signal is bad in parts of Pizzo, and especially in the house we are in, so I went out to get the signal outside. I texted Maria to explain this, asking her to call me then, or to send an email with the appointed time to meet. She did not call back so I went in and waited for an email. It did not arrive within half an hour so we went out to be able to receive a call from Maria or to make one. We went for cappuccini in Ercole's Gelateria. He seems to like to talk to us and Donna seems to like him and his place. The waiter, who had claimed to me to be German, talked of the match against Spain and Italy being gone. I asked him was he the son of the owner of Bar Ercole. He denied it but Donna seemed to catch him out. We had a laugh and he seems up "for the crack" (ready for a laugh and some slagging), as we say in Ireland. I was waiting for the phone call from Maria and yet, when it came I didn't get to it on time. I called her myself and she said she could not get to us today and would meet us tomorrow morning. She did offer to have us meet Alessia again, who was in Pizzo with clients, but said we probably needed her, Maria, for the issues we needed to discuss. We agreed.

Donna offered to go shopping on her own up on Via Nazionale and I was glad not to have to climb those steps again as my legs and knees were still sore from the previous day. I went back at 12.00 approximately to let her in as we only had one key. I also texted Francesco to thank him for the lift to tennis the night before and for getting us into the courts. Donna had bought burgers and she cooked for the first time here. They were fine and I had a salad to go with them. My beach chair, on which I was sitting, collapsed under me, however, but luckily I was not hurt really.

In the afternoon it was off to the cove nearby, used by fishermen. I had my swim but it was too hot there and we had no umbrella so Donna suggested going around to the marina, where she had an ice cream for the first time here. She says they don't really agree with her but enjoyed it anyway. We also got our first lift back on the tourist train, running out to him as he came into the marina and he stopped for us on the way back. He had offered the day before. We are definitely getting "in" here in Pizzo, becoming real Pizzitani.

Dermot, our son, was on skype when we went on the internet and contacted us. His house, which he bought and moved into a month or two ago, is being refurbished too and is nearly finished. He is staying in our house in Dublin at present with Nicola and Lily, their daughter. It was great to see and talk to him and her. He had to go to his house to deal with something but we got to see and talk to Nicola, who told us Lily had a kidney complaint, but she looked fine. Their house is nearly ready for them to move back into. Anna and Liam will be happy to move into our house then, to mind it for us while we are away. We are a busy family!

Donna got dressed up to go to the piazza and have a stroll around. She had her first "gelato tartufo" in Ercole's and enjoyed it. I find it too rich for me and had a bowl of assorted ice creams and some fruit. We just relaxed and chatted to Sandro and Sara, who had introduced themselves to us at the Italian match on Sunday. They offered to bring us to another town where music was available. They seem very friendly and we agreed to meet them at the next match to make arrangements. Donna had mentioned getting alici but, when we went to the trattoria where I had got them before, they were not on the menu.

However, it had been another good day, a day of many firsts and I like such days. We were also getting reports of terrible weather in Ireland and elsewhere in Europe so Pizzo, and its heat wave, we were very happy with.

MERCOLEDI 25 GIUGNO

Maria arrived at about 10.45 in the piazza in a white suit and we did not recognise her. Donna went after her to check and brought her back to where I was sitting, first asking her about Alessio. He was in London and Donna got the latest low-down on the state of play there. We did not want to pry but we did have an interest, as he had promised us our house would be ready by 1 June and I had asked for him to be involved again, as he was an architect and could argue our case more strongly with Mr Plant. He also has to keep an eye on the work and report to me, as he had done some weeks ago.

Maria first of all sorted out some bank details, especially with Donna, but also with me and it was opportune because I had tried to withdraw money from the ATM machines around the piazza and had failed for some reason. I did not think I had exceeded my monthly limit but maybe I had and she said she could have it raised anyway. Next I launched into my issues about the house and what attitude we should take with Paolo. She listened and agreed about not paying for more accommodation as the house was not ready, his responsibility. As regards the window replacing the back door she said she would have to take a look, but I felt we should be adamant on it being replaced, as we had not been consulted on any change and we wanted a door there. I went through the rest of my demands and enquiries, as per the email I had sent Alessia, which seemingly she or Maria had not seen, being unable to open the Word document attached, a very strange occurrence!

We went up to the house and met Paolo there. The door issue was the first issue raised and Paolo said he had consulted Alessio on it and it was part of the detailed plan for that area. Seemingly, Alessio had not informed us of this and also it would be difficult to change now as much work had been done and a toilet bowl was to go in front of where the door had been. A shower, washing machine and toilet had to go in a very small area and discussion got heated at times, me sticking to my guns, and Paolo maintaining his position. Maria was trying to sort it out. I suggested Paolo come back to us with a new plan but Maria said it would have to done there and then, as we did not want any more delays. She was quite right about that and I was glad she kept at it because we worked out a plan whereby the toilet bowl did not have to be moved and a small door could be fitted. Paolo and Maria were also worried about such a door on the ground floor for security reasons but we said we were happy to take that chance. It is usual to have strong, even reinforced doors, on the ground floor in Italy, it seems. I feel Pizzo is quite safe and anyway an outer, metal or heavy door can always be added later.

I was glad we had forced the issue and was happy to accept Paolo's assurances of doing his best, while he expressed himself sorry for the delay on the completion of the house.

"Mister P-O-W-E-R," he said, lengthening my name seriously, "He angry with me"

I said that I had to be firm and stand up for myself, especially on this issue. Donna told him

"He is Irish, he gets angry with me too", and tried to reassure him.

Later, when discussing the area behind the terrace, where we were going to put a bed, he said, in Italian, the words of which I cannot remember, but the gist was

"You can sleep here when there is a row!"

My wife jumped in to tell him I would be thrown over the terrace in such an event. Lovely!

He had felt, he said, that I was angry with him but I assured him I trusted him to do a good, even a beautiful job and we shook hands many times to show our mutual trust. I know, as Maria said, that Paolo is staking his considerable reputation on doing good work and he wanted to let us know it. Also, few would have taken on the job, it seems. Maria blamed her husband, Alessio, for the lack of consultation and I agreed with her, but said we were the ones suffering as a result, and we had to be firm and demand good standards and fair play. Things got easier after that, with many compromises being made. I accepted that another recess could not be made into a window and that the terrace wall could not be removed and replaced by a railing. Paolo agreed to allow us to stay in his mother's house without further payment, until our house was ready and completed, after Maria backed him into a corner, both literally and metaphorically. A bidet, which I had wanted, would be installed in the shower room on the first floor. Paolo said it was because I was becoming very Italian, as he said, and that many English do not demand them. I took it as a compliment. I complimented him on various features, like the stone wall left bare but treated, in the double bedroom and elsewhere, and I liked some little recesses, Italian style, which he had incorporated. Bright colours, simplicity, aesthetic values, design elements and natural lights had been my guidelines and he had agreed to try and achieve that and had already done so. The stairs was also sorted out. I had expressed a desire for a wooden one but we agreed with the basic metal one, which could be upgraded later. I wanted to keep further costs down and just get the job done and had felt his prices for wooden stairs were excessive. He invited me to go to a showroom with him but we left it at the original stairs as was in the first plan and contract. We did ask about improving the path in front of the house and were told the council, or Commune di Pizzo, would have to give permission. Many other smaller issues were likewise settled and Maria noted everything and got us to sign an agreed version later at a bar.

I had to go back to our apartment to get some bank papers so Maria could get Donna's bank card activated and joined them afterwards. I was glad we had sorted out so much, even though the house would still not be ready until 20 July. In Italy, and indeed in Ireland and England, builders often did not finish jobs on time. It is not unusual. The cordial relations maintained would make it easier for us to meet and talk to Paolo again. He invited us to come and see the work and said we would understand better how difficult it was to work in such heat and the access difficulties, which I knew already.

There were some light moments too as when Paolo said he wanted to meet our daughters. This was a playful, yet quite serious request, I felt, and a way of expressing his admiration for Donna's beauty and personality in general, I knew. We promised to have a party in Pizzo and invite him to Dublin. He is young and would be a good "catch", but I think he may be married already, if not too sure about the strength of his commitment! He had also wanted to be praised and had pointed out how he had enlarged the terrace and other features he felt good about. I was happy to do that. I do think we will have a fine house when it is finished and Donna did say later she felt much happier about it.

Afterwards, Maria brought us to Lamezia, where she was able to activate Donna's ATM card and then she kindly drove us back to the train station. We went to Vibo Marina then, to find out if we could hire a canoe, kayak or boat for when Bernard, Mark and Anna came. It was the mezzogiorno and everywhere was shut, except for the bars. We had a meal in one. The tourist office was near and we enquired there when it opened. They could not help really and had little English but we got a phone number we could try and we left it at that.

We were tired but made our way to the marina in Pizzo, after getting the train back and noting times of trains from Pizzo station. The tourist train picked us up and almost brought us home. Thank God and Frank, the driver, for us being accepted as "Pizzitani".

A good day's work had been done and progress, although slow, was being made. Our dream of a home in Pizzo was that bit closer. I looked over old emails and found that it was around this time last year we had first heard of the house in Via Campanella, on 24 July 2007 to be exact. Hopefully, we would be taking possession of it by that date in 2008. We will have realised our dream in less than a year, if so.

JOVEDI 26 GIUGNO

After the high of the day before, today seemed an anti-climax. We went to the weekly market up on Via Nazionale. Donna felt a little out of sorts again, homesickness setting in maybe. We did buy some stuff for our house and the one we were staying in. We were going to be there for another 3 weeks at least. Donna also put her clothes away. She had been still living out of her case. We did a clean up also.

Our routine changed slightly as we went to the beach early and stayed longer from about 2 pm to almost 5 pm. The "trenino" (little tourist train) lift back was great as my bad knee seemed to be giving me more pain than usual, with me waking in the night with it getting stiff and sore. The driver Frank called us over that night, when we were walking in the piazza, to ask Donna in Italian why she, being so beautiful, went around with this old man. I just burst out laughing, understanding him quicker than Donna, to whom I had to explain it. I had heard him use "bella donna" for her and "vecchio" for me. That was enough. I am used to such sentiments although they are not usually expressed so forcibly or directly at me. I am not so much older than her, six years in fact. She does look younger and amazing for someone who had seven children. She often jokes herself that she married an older man, especially when I am bringing up old songs, ancient history (from the fifties) or stories. I regularly get slagging like this and do not get upset. Maybe I should. It is just part of the deal, I suppose, when you marry a beautiful woman and I can take it most times.

Before that Donna, who had been feeling a bit low and told me, went to see the restaurant where I had asked about her learning "Cucina Italiana". Katarina and Anthony, the people I had spoken to, were there and welcomed us. They were still happy to have her and to help her and she was still interested. She was feeling a bit down and thought if she got involved in something and distracted herself she would be better off. I had tried to do that the first few days she was in Pizzo when she had felt likewise and now she was doing it herself, which I was glad to see. She said she didn't really want to go back to Ireland. It was raining there and she knew she would be sorry if she did. It was part of the new stage of her life, now that our children had grown and she had to learn to live for herself and do things. Her mother had also died last year and it was hard on her and she was trying to adjust. Next week we would be going to our Italian lessons and we checked out the website. Donna also wanted to do a ceramics course and there was one advertised. Learning by doing is very much her style. So there were things to look forward to and people to meet.

I also enquired about hiring a car for the day to bring Bernard, Olive and Anna Marie to Naples airport for their return flight. We had been considering changing our return flight too, and going with them from Naples instead of Rome. Donna thought it might be better to go on the train to Rome for all of us and was thinking of suggesting it to Bernard but we were checking out our options. Hiring a car for a day in Pizzo I had found out only cost about €50 but not for going to Naples. An internet quotation I got mentioned $212, which seemed excessive and I replied to it in those terms. It was not until September anyway and we could check it out a bit more.

We finished the day by watching Spain beat Russia by 3-0. I was delighted the Spanish won as their skill and creativity was greater. I hoped they would beat a hard-working but not as skilful German team. They would be my new favourite team now that Italy were out. A win for them would be good for good football, I feel.

VENERDI 27 GIUGNO

Donna went to the restaurant where we had talked to some people the night before and they had said they were willing to let her see and learn about Italian cooking. I had gone to the piazza with her and we had a cappuccino first. Then she went on and I went to buy some milk and prosciutto crudo. I decided to take Paolo's advice and go and have a look at the work so I bought some cold water and some polpetti (like meat balls) for the workers. The shop assistant had not got change for me so told me to pay later. It speaks volumes of how I was being trusted I think, but maybe everybody is treated like this in Pizzo. The workers in the house were glad of what I brought, I think, just remarking it was hot. Yes, working in a heat wave like we were having, was not the best. I had a look around and left them to it.

Later, Donna returned as the arrangement was not really satisfactory for some people. The older man working had taken exception to another body in his space maybe and it is easy to see that, as there was little space. He may have been stressed also and the arrival of the police, for some reason, meant the lady who had been so kind to let her in had to ask her to go. One can see it might not have been a good idea for all sorts of reasons, including Donna's own welfare and the effect on the rest of the staff, especially if anything went wrong. She had given it a try, as had the kind lady who took her on, but it was not really appropriate.

On reading her emails, Donna discovered that Frances, our daughter in Australia, was looking for money. She had been looking for a job and had not been successful and the camper van, which had proved more costly than expected, was up for sale but had no takers. We had ignored all hints for money previously but felt we had to relent this time. She would not have asked directly if she was not in real straits. She is tough and proud.

I emailed her back to say we would send money, sounding as light-hearted about it as I could, but told her we would have to search for a Western Union place in Pizzo, which might be difficult. It proved to be so.

First I went to the tourist office, "Pro Loco", but the guy said he did not know of one in the town. I suggested the post office might have such a service and he thought it might be worth a try. It didn't but I was given some directions, in Italian, to shops which might have it, after some dialogue broke out between the lady in the post office and the customers. I understood little of this but got her to write down the addresses she suggested. There was one out at "Piedigrotta" where we had gone a few days ago. I thought I might get the little train out but it was nearly one o'clock now and it might be closed by the time I got there. I texted Donna and she said to wait until 4pm. Frank, the tourist train driver, had not been very interested and said later would be better. Not having Donna with me may have been a factor too, just maybe! I had a beer at the Pantheon Bar and paid for the shopping I had got earlier. My having a drink was spotted by another gentleman whom we met later at night and he said it to Donna. I had been reported on!

At about 3.30 I started "googling" western union to find their outlets in Pizzo. I found three and one of them in Pizzo near our house had been mentioned by the lady in the post office. Another was supposed to be on Via Nazionale. Otherwise, we would have to go to the one near Piedigrotta. We had been going to get a bus to it but decided to try the others which had come up on Google. We walked up to the first, which was halfway up the hill, found the shop, but it did not offer a Western Union service, if it ever had. On to Via Nazionale, where the same was the case. Now we were left with the one near the grotto. We had missed the bus and decided to walk. It was all downhill, but in some heat, and we even tried to hitch but failed. We got there only to be asked for our passports which we did not have. Donna did have her driving licence and this was accepted finally, after some phone calls. We did the business and left, getting a hitch back, which was great. Once a parent, always a parent, was a thought which sprang to mind but it was no use complaining. We had signed on for the job quite willingly. I just wished it did not entail unexpected pleasures like we just had. They were only little problems really, if one judges by many other people's experiences. To find out later there was a Western Union agent about 100 metres from our house, only made us feel a little stunned and foolish but it gave us a laugh too.

Donna found a wedding proceeding in the church near us and went to have a look. I tried to text my daughter to tell her the money had been sent but my credit was gone and it delayed that effort, but eventually she got the message. Everything seems to go at the same time, doesn't it? Donna's credit was gone too. We had tried to phone Frances on skype but she was not available. The phone signal did not allow me to get calls or messages on my Italian phone. I got quite tired and frustrated.

At night we went to meet Sandro and Sara who had introduced

themselves to us when we were watching a match a few days earlier. They were very friendly and Sandro had promised to bring us out of Pizzo to a nice restaurant by the sea where they had music often but not that night. These nights are frequent only in July and August. We met Sara first in the piazza as Sandro was playing billiards somewhere, she said. We had a drink and a talk and when he came we went to his car and he drove us out by Marinella. He showed us the Western Union agency, which was not very far from where we were living! We had a good laugh about that. The restaurant was on the beach and had an extensive outdoor area, with space for musical events and dancing, games and other amusements. We sat by the beach and enjoyed the fresh sea breeze and the quiet relaxing mood of the evening.

They told us about themselves and we did likewise, sharing family news and jokes. Their attitude to life was relaxed and they were roughly our age; their only son was grown up, just like our children. Sandro invited us to choose antipasti and our main meal. We had wine and beer and settled into a great night. Afterwards, he got up and I suspected he was going to pay so I jumped up to prevent him and to offer. He said he was only going to the toilet but he did pay and when later I went to pay I was told it was all settled. I couldn't believe such kindness and friendliness. In Ireland we consider ourselves hospitable and think we are so welcoming but this was amazing to me. I thanked him, of course, but it seemed a very feeble gesture on my part to me. Later we drove back to the piazza and had another drink, which I allowed to pay for. Sara was getting sleepy and we would have gone but Sandro launched into a story of how an American girl, who originally came from Pizzo had tried to marry him. He was often on cruises in America and used meet her but nothing came of it. Another gentleman also joined us and bent Donna's ear quite a lot with how well respected in the town I was! He had another story to tell of how he got married and separated to a local girl who now lives in Australia. A great night was had and stories followed stories and we were very happy with all the friends and connections we had made. This town is so friendly!

SABATO 28 GIUGNO

I just wanted this day to be normal and relaxed and so it was. No running around in the heat of the midday sun, putting pressure on myself to get something done, like I had had yesterday. We got up late. I had needed a good sleep. We phoned Frances on skype to make sure she had got the money and she had, as well as another bar job. We went to the piazza for a cappuccino and to buy daily supplies.

I wrote up my diary and decided four weeks of a diary was enough and I would return to normal chapters to finish the book and to honour the title "The Year of Buying a House in Italy", my original choice of name for this book. The year would be up soon and the finishing line was in sight. Anyway, maybe four weeks was enough to give a flavour of the life we were living............... and going to live.

I emailed some chapters to my family asking for their comments and Donna asked Bernard to consider going changing his flight home from Naples to Rome. The flight from Naples is about 11am in the day and it is impossible to get a train from here to get there on time on the day. My idea of hiring a car did not appeal to my wife, or maybe it was my driving, and it was going to be more expensive than at first thought.

The beach beckoned, as I had not had a swim for two days! It was great getting in (and back to normal in Pizzo). We bought fresh "alici" (sardines) and cooked them in the oven and they were very tasty. Another new discovery and another first!

We intended to stay in and not go to the piazza but at about 9.15 pm Donna suggested going for a walk on the lower road, the one the cars use coming up from the beach and the castle. We did, and heard music coming from a local bar. I had not brought any money with me, so Donna went back to get some and we went in for a drink. It was high above cliffs at the cove the fishermen used and at this time of night it looked very romantic with lights and fine table settings, in such a dramatic landscape. A few people were sitting and many others soon arrived. The music came from a man on a keyboard and he interspersed his Italian songs with hits from the charts of the 60's, 70's and so on. Slow romantic songs, like we had been looking for and we loved the place, Donna suggesting we go there for our wedding anniversary in August. We would have loved to have tasted the food but a booking would have been necessary and I was certainly not dressed up for the occasion, having just slipped out for a walk (with my swimming togs on back the front!). We had our beer and prosecco and drank in the lovely intimate atmosphere. It was a perfect end to a relaxing Italian day. Well almost……….that came later!

SUNDAY 29 JUNE

Donna today decided to do the tourist thing so we went to the castle which rises up from the marina and is situated at the end the main piazza. It is hundreds of years old and has seen many changes in its history. It is called Murat's Castle and there is a museum and lots of interesting information to be gleaned from it. The Spanish, French and Neapolitans have all occupied it and it was an important fort on the Mediterranean. On the 13th. October 1815 J.Murat, King of Naples and Napoleon's brother-in-law, was imprisoned, sentenced and finally shot here for trying to instigate rebellion.

That night was the final of the European Nations Cup and we had a great time with the crowd who mostly supported Germany while I shouted for Spain. They had impressed me with their vision, speed and style of play and I was very glad they had won. It would be good for football I thought. The final was not as well attended in the piazza as the Italian match against Spain but I suppose that is only natural. Most people seemed to be up for Germany or expected them to win but I stuck my neck out and supported Spain as I felt they had played the better football generally and needed some success to reward them, much as I admire Germany and have always rated them. I bet on them in the 1974 world cup to win and I don't usually gamble. I did not back Spain with my money this time but that is not unusual. I seemed to be almost alone cheering for them and when I asked Sandro why this was the case he said it was because Spain had beaten Italy, not a very good reason in my book or really credible. The fact that the Germans were admired for being winners, I felt, was the more likely reason. I enjoyed the game more than most and left, happy that the best football team had won and it would be best for football itself. Torres had shown great skill and pace to score and it was a fitting end to his season.

MONDAY 30 JUNE

Today we started our Italian classes, which we had booked back in January. There was only one other student which was not great. However, we did get individual attention but only for 1 hour instead of the two we expected. It was enough as it is very intensive. We were offered various trips and activities but decided against as there were only three of us. That night we did go to see a film shown by the teacher, Antonio, in the apartment where we had had our lesson.

How did you like the diary? It was getting boring writing it every day so I stopped but I hope it gave you a feel for what daily life was like for me and my wife for the first few weeks in Pizzo. Much of it was just that, an account of going swimming, eating in or out, taking lessons, but events also occurred and we had to sort out our feelings about living here and buying the house while dealing with the joys of it and coping with the delays, decisions and difficulties which arose.

The best part for me was of the soccer tournament I had been enjoying since I came to Pizzo almost. It had almost kept me going at times. I met some great people through watching it and it had been a great introduction to the locals and helped a lot later on.

We had booked Italian lessons so on Monday 30 June we went to an apartment up on Via Nazionale. I was tested and assessed as being not exactly a beginner and Donna started as a beginner. Ivano, my teacher, was good but talked too much Italian. It made lessons too difficult and with nobody else to bounce off it was too intensive, especially on the first day. Social activities had been planned but with only two other students at other levels it was not the best. I did not return the following week as I had intended. Donna took up a ceramics course which she enjoyed but it proved very expensive.

CHAPTER 8

"With hills serene about you like a crown
And at your feet, the solemn-sounding sea!"

Giosue Carducci

JULY
Delays and Progress

Pizzo is a small town on the coast of Calabria, south of Naples, near Vibo Valentia. The centro storico is situated high above the promenade. The piazza is the main square at the side of the historic Murat's Castle and is the focal point of the life of the town and of every celebration. On all sides of it there are gelateria (ice cream bars +), bars, shops, restaurants and all with seating stretching into the Piazza flanked by tall buildings. There is a defunct hotel (newly opened in 2009 as a B&B) and a church also. Traffic in and out of the piazza is highly regulated during the summer, especially at night. The main tourist shopping street, or corso, leads off it at the end of the piazza opposite the castle and there are several other streets also, one leading up to the newer, more modern town and its main thoroughfare, Via Nazionale, with supermarkets, garages, and the principal road leading north and south. Many Pizzitani have moved from the centro storico to this area of modern apartments and convenience shopping. The local market is held off Via Nazionale every Thursday and buses can be seen snaking through here then, and at other busy times. There is a local bus down to the rail station and to and from Marinella, a seaside resort to the north, and Vibo Valentia, the principal market town to the south inland, as well as other less frequent ones. In summer more buses are put into service and cater for those going to the beach, although they are not always very reliable, as we found. A private bus (which has the appearance of a train engine), the pizzo express, started to operate this year in summer and has been very successful, going to Piedagrotto church with the statues carved out of the cliff and which has its interior being renewed. This "Piedigrotta" is one of a number of local tourist attractions along with the castle. Of course, there are churches everywhere, such as the one which was ruined in a minor earth tremor and restored by the people. A plaque outside shows them carrying bricks and blocks to help rebuild it. It is especially famous for its devotion to San Francesco di Paola, and is situated at the other end of the tourist shopping street which leads to the main piazza. Many other streets and alleys, each one higher up than the previous one, lead up to the main road, Via Nazionale. The autostrada and main rail lines are not far away, making for easy access north and south, north to Naples and Rome or south to Reggio Calabria. In fact, Pizzo was considered to be a little Naples and thus named Napitia for a long time and is linked to it by the castle among other factors.

"Pizzo" in Italian means a beak, and so means "dip my beak in the sauce or money", an Italian colloquialism for protection money which gave us cause to worry for a while but we had no problems in that regard. Maybe we just lived on the surface above the mean realities of daily life but we were not anxious to discover them. We were enjoying ourselves and escaping our reality back home in Ireland where life was not turning out so well. Ireland had just given the Lisbon Treaty a surprising "No" and confounded our European partners. The weather there was atrocious for summer also. We were glad to escape it. However, it was not just for a holiday we came but to get our house finished and to move in. That was proving difficult. Below is an account from that time…………………

It is 21 July, the day after the third deadline to complete the house has passed and the house is still a long way from completion. I cannot relax or decide what to do and how to work it out. First of all, panic set in on Friday last when Maria and Alessio, the agents I was using to buy the house and get the work done, said I would have to pay more fees or they would not provide their services any more. I had questioned an invoice sent to me the previous

Wednesday. After some emails and phone calls back and forth Maria sent me this text

"I am not willing to take any further action or spend any further money on your behalf if I am not paid for my services. I do this for a living ....etc"

With the delay in getting the house done I really need all the help I can get at this time. I understood when I paid the fees to Maria on completion of the purchase (3 June) with the notaio, that I had paid all the fees expected and I would continue to receive their services until the works were finished as I had paid a percentage of the total cost of the deal and of the works agreed on the house. Now she wants to be paid for translations, visits, phone calls and other services that were included in the service before the completion of the purchase of the house. As well as that it seems her husband wants to be paid separately for his visits and his overseeing of the work. I thought all this was included in the fee I had paid. We had exchanged emails about all this and both sides were getting "hot under the collar". I was questioning the fees and she was saying if I didn't pay she would have no more to do with me, at a time when I needed help badly. I texted her and her husband and, after some curt replies and "stonewalling" on their part and my efforts to get them back on course, they agreed to meet me on the Monday after the deadline had passed. They had originally been part of a team and had now separated which probably added to the complications

At this stage what exactly was not done? This long list I made out about this time

- No doors
- No windows
- Ground floor not even started as regards cement floor, tiling etc
- No toilets, showers, sinks, bidet, water tank, water heater, etc
- Men who had been promised to do the tiling had not arrived and the usual guys were doing it and so could not do the other

work. I had been promised other workers, specialists in tiling, would arrive to do it.

- Painting only done on 2 outside walls
- Mounds of rubbish and rubble still outside and our neighbours had moved in
- Electrics not done
- 2 sets of stairs not in

There was probably more I didn't even know about but I had enough to worry about there. I had a few sleepless nights around this time between the lack of progress and the row over fees. My mood was not the best during the day either and I am sure it was not easy on my wife, who seemed more relaxed about it.

A nervous man it was, therefore, who met Maria and Alessio on Monday 21 July, but, thankfully, we went straight away to the house on Alessio's suggestion to deal with Mr.Plant and the work delays. Donna did not come with me deciding it would be better to leave us to it. Fees were not even mentioned initially as if there had been no problem, for which I was very grateful. Maria went off quite early in the proceedings which got me worried also and Mr.Plant had taken an hour to arrive which did not help. However, Alessio had a good look around and pronounced himself happy with the work so far but not with the pace of the work. He said it would take another two weeks. I let him deal with Mr.Plant apart from interjecting that I could not believe Mr.Plant's word or promises any more and I know I was being very cynical and getting him irritated.

"Non posso credere lui" (I cannot believe him) I said, which got Mr.Plant's back up but I felt he deserved it at that time.

Alessio was patient and yet firm with him and got assurances about the arrival of stairs and other items. Mr.Plant said many jobs would only take a day to do and would be done by the very people who delivered items such as the doors, windows, etc. Alessio got their phone numbers and promised to ring them himself. He had Mr.Plant under pressure and I left them to it eventually and Alessio stayed to inspect the preparatory work they were doing on the stairs from the ground floor up, the first steps of which were being built up with tufo stone. At one stage Alessio injected a bit of humour saying he would kill Mr.Plant if I wished but who would get the work done then? I needed some relief as I was very angry but that was no use. In the end I accepted their assurances that it would be finished in two or three weeks. The workers were going on holidays on 9 August so it would have to be. He did tell me also that Mr.Plant was sorry he had sold me the house and he would have been interested in calling off the deal if he could, because he saw it was bigger and better than he had realised and he could get a lot more for it. The stairs arrived the next morning which helped to improve matters and Mr.Plant reminded me that I had not believed him. Cordial relations were established again. I had felt all along it would be done well and be aesthetically pleasing as well, and wanted Mr.Plant to succeed in this, so I had to be patient and a bit more laid-back, Italian style. I find it hard when plans are not put into action or promises kept. I would have to learn. Maria and Alessio got their money as I needed their help in getting the house done although I was not too happy to have to pay more than I had expected. They had also caused us problems with their marriage break-up but these are the problems life throws up and they were not successful in restoring the relationship and indeed I was sad for them. The latest news I have is that their business relationship is no more either.

As the bus driver said to us once, "Noi siamo in Italia!" (We are in Italy!), when we were asking about a bus not arriving according to schedule. It was a lesson in Italian life, especially down south, a philosophical outlook I would have to take on board as otherwise life would be very fraught and I would not be able to live for a lengthy period here and relax and enjoy it, which was the point of the whole exercise.

The workers were Bulgarian twins and I did not have a problem with them. Some people had told me they were slow and not the best but they seemed to work hard as far as I could see. I encouraged them, of course, bringing them snacks and large bottles of "acqua frizzante freda (cold fizzy water)" every so often. I also turned a blind eye to some strange occurrences. Another Bulgarian who worked now and then told me the house would be finished in two weeks and I got encouragement from that, at what was a difficult time for us. Mr.Plant's father did a lot of work on the house also but I found conversation with him difficult to understand, although he was helpful in many ways. He also came to the house we were staying in, which belonged to his wife, we were told, to solve some of our problems.

During June Maria had suggested we might use an interior decorator to get furniture for our house. He came with Alessia, one day in June, to measure rooms and to get some ideas. Later he gave us his proposals but we found them too expensive and managed to get or order our own for about a third of his price. The standard may not have been as good but costs were escalating and it was to be only a summer holiday house for us and we were not willing to spend much more.

We had expected to be in the house by then, but we had believed Mr.Plant when he had said it would be finished by 20 July, or maybe we just wanted to believe it. We had many decisions to make. For instance, he wanted us to get certain tiles but the price was putting us off. We decided to just get plain white everywhere at first as a result, but later I was thinking about it and relented, unable to accept such plainness and I rang Mr.Plant who agreed to lower the price as he also wanted to make the house a showcase for his work and he was afraid it wouldn't do his reputation any good if people came and saw plain white everywhere. I felt better after changing my mind and was also reassured about Mr.Plant and his sense of the aesthetic. He wanted a beautiful house for us, as well as for himself.

We had to buy furniture for the house and a kitchen was a priority. Our friends Sandro and Sara brought us to a big store, "Trony", and we were happy with the prices and ordered a fitted kitchen which would be delivered in August. We also got other stuff like a double bed, divans and a washing machine.

At the beginning of July we were starting our Italian classes, having a holiday together and just making decisions about the house mostly. We went on various outings with the teacher such as to a beach near Zambrone train station called "Paradise Beach" (and it was beautiful, but hard work to get to, across fields and down an often steep clay path), also to see a film, and to have a meal together.

We enjoyed ourselves making new friends and getting to know Pizzo better. Sandro and Sara continued to look after us in many ways. Sandro came one day with a huge, hot, freshly-made lasagne he had cooked for our lunch. Another day he organised a van to transport our washing machine and also sorted out a delivery problem with a divan, even coming down to the beach to collect us to get it into the house where we were staying after it had been delivered to our new unfinished house. The stray cats would have mess a mess of it there he said, as the windows and doors were not yet in.

Another group of friends we made were English-speaking and were involved in setting up a business in Pizzo related to property, an internet café, an English language newsletter and many other ventures. Paul, Lorraine, Leon and Beata of Calabrian Investg had been involved in business in Spain together and had decided to leave it and try their luck in Pizzo. I had asked them for help as regards sending money by Western Union and they were very friendly and we all got to know each other quite well. I wrote some articles for the newsletter and got great help from them on many fronts. We also met many Irish couples, all of whom seemed to be interested in buying in Pizzo and we were able to give them the benefit of out experiences and even show them our house, unfinished as it was. It was great to have conversation in English at times, although we were still anxious to improve our Italian. It did require more effort and still does but the ease of talking English can become very attractive at times.

In fact, I even started an English language conversation group in the Pantheon Bar on Monday nights. I had advertised for English language students almost immediately I came to Pizzo, by way of flyers I created on my computer and printer. They were not very successful despite being translated into Italian for me by Angela, Marco and Laura, who worked in the tourist office and who also made good suggestions. No students arrived so the idea of starting a conversation group arose to get people interested in learning English and also to provide us English speakers with a social outlet on a regular basis. Few Italians turned up and as an exchange it didn't really work but it was a good night out for us English speakers. We had more than ten people the first night; some tourists, some locals, and some who had bought property in Pizzo or were in the process of doing so. A young girl, Carmen, who was working in the bar for the summer and who was studying English in Messina university was very interested and helped us with our Italian, as did another prospective student of mine who also played tennis, Francesco. He got us into the local tennis courts too. He was a very busy investment banker who wanted to learn English but had little time. We had hoped to attract many of the young locals who were studying English but few came. We met some on a bus one day and knew there were many more but, it being summer, they did not come to the group as they were either studying for upcoming exams in September, working for the summer or just relaxing on the beach and elsewhere. The group met about four or five times before it fizzled out in August when the big tourist numbers came in and it may have been impossible to run it anyway.

We tried out various beaches such as Seggiola, Pranji and the one near the train station. Seggiola was a bay made famous by Cicero and now used for boats and fishing mostly. It was quiet and not a tourist beach. Some locals swam there and also did diving and snorkelling. My friend Sandro had a friend working there on the boats and he allowed me out rowing one day. It was really my first time and I was quite nervous but I stayed inside the marina area and even convinced Donna to come on board the second time I rowed out. The ducks and ducklings were to be seen there too and we watched their progress with interest.

The weekly market in Pizzo on a Thursday was worth a regular visit and we also made our way to Vibo Valentia, where a much bigger market was held on Saturdays. The usual stalls selling household goods, food such as meat, cheese, fruit and vegetables, farm produce, clothes, detergents and beauty products, shoes and trinkets were to be found. In Vibo it was a huge affair but much the same as Pizzo. The pedestrian corso in Vibo was interesting and a pleasure to walk also with its more usual fashion and department stores, book shops with English books and much more. The coffee shops and gelateria were very convenient for me when my wife wanted to browse. Sandro brought us there first but we did get there by bus as well.

I bought my man bag in Pizzo and still have it but am not sure of wearing it in Ireland although it is a very handy way to mind one's phone, wallet, change, and other essentials. Maybe I am thinking of the time my friend arrived back from Germany to my wedding over 35 years ago with his man bag and we gave him a terrible time. Time has moved on but not sufficiently for me to try it out in Dublin.

I did my writing and went on the internet usually about midday to keep me inside, during the hottest part of the day. Shops closed and the piazza was usually deserted at that time although bars and gelateria stayed open. We did some simple cooking or had a salad for lunch usually. We were in contact with family members in

Ireland and with Frances, our daughter in Australia through emails and my wife's Bebo site, on which we put photos of our holiday in Pizzo. There were some problems with our internet connection, especially with Skype but it was successful if we just used text or phone messages. Our other daughter was getting married on 24 July, 2009, and by coincidence that was the date when we had viewed our Pizzo house in 2007.

CHAPTER 9

**"It is August now,
I have hoped but I hope no more.. "
(Patrick Kavanagh)**

Moving In

In the poem above Paddy Kavanagh is referring to a beech tree he has planted and which has not succeeded in growing. Unlike the poem, it was not that I had to give up hope because of failure, but success! I didn't have to hope any more because my house was finally completed and I moved into it! On 9 August I was able to sleep there at last and start to live there! The week before I moved in had been a very strange one as my wife was back in Ireland and I had been feeling very lonely and emotional at times. But the house had kept me going. I don't think it would have ever been finished if I had not been here. Stories of people waiting years for work to be completed abounded, especially if they could only come over for two weeks or so every year to check up on it. Everyday in the first week of August another section of the work on the house was completed. I had always felt it would it work out in the end but it was great to actually see it happening at close range.

A cement floor was laid and the floor tiling done on the ground floor one day. Another day the sanitary goods arrived and were installed in the toilets and shower rooms. The downstairs shower room was tiled, both walls and floors. Electricity and water was provided and all the necessary work involved was finished with. The balcony was tiled and sorted another day and painting both inside and outside was completed and the scaffolding taken down. More furniture arrived for me successfully. Many other final details were attended to and I moved in on Saturday, 9 August, as I really wanted to, even though there were a few jobs outstanding, like the installation of internal doors. The workers and I celebrated by having a few beers and some food. I had asked them to come to a bar but they wouldn't enter one in their dirty working clothes so I brought some beer and food to them. They were going on holiday to Bulgaria on Monday and had their own reasons for celebrating. We conversed as best we could due to my "poco Italiano" and they told me they themselves had arrived with none of the language a few years previously.

It was strange sleeping in the house that night but I could not wait any longer. With no internal doors and no door into our part of the house, at the top of the communal stairs I shared with my neighbour, I didn't exactly feel safe and had many sleepless moments, hearing noises and being kept awake, mostly due to my own nervousness, but I had wanted for so long to do this. The next day was a Sunday but one of the workers, who was not going on holiday, came to finish some final work and his wife came to help me clean the place. They got something done but there was still plenty left for me to do later. I slept in the room behind the terrace on the second floor but it was still very hot. The next few nights I tried the first floor room with the balcony which was a bit better.

One night shortly after moving in, I was woken about 2 am by a drunken English man who was locked out and very angry about it. He cursed his friend for locking him out and uttered terrible threats, banging on the door and losing his temper, along with his phone and other items, I guess. He kept at it for about 2 hours and must have tried to climb up but fell and cut himself and was bleeding. I had doubts about my wisdom in buying there that night. I actually met him later with his friend at a dinner to which we were all invited. He seemed ok and I did not mention the incident. He and his friends left the next day but he arrived back in September.

Each day after I moved in, I had plenty to do. I swept and washed the tiles repeatedly. There was furniture to be assembled which I was quite glad to do and enjoyed the concentration it required of me and the joy of getting it done. One item, a wardrobe with a mirror on front defeated me as I had got the wrong package of instructions and screws, nuts and bolts etc to go with it. I phoned the shop and was assured they would ring back but, of course, they didn't. It was sorted out eventually, with some help from a friend. I did manage to assemble a divan, a base storage unit and a table and four chairs without too much difficulty. Cleaning up after builders was the real problem with cement stains on the tiles and the new grouting spreading a grey dust everywhere even after being mopped, or maybe because of it!.

There was the thrill of sitting on my balcony, emailing, reading or writing. Yes, I even had one beer one day just in order to send a photo of the event home but for a while I was off the beer as I had felt a bit down, when my wife had left to return to Ireland to work for some weeks, before returning with my son and daughter and their boy/girl friends. Eating my own food in my house also added to the joy of the experience and getting and preparing it, even without a fitted kitchen. I enjoyed the whole experience of doing my own thing in my own house in Italy, which we had dreamed about for years.

But I was lonely now without my wife. She had to go back to Ireland on 2 August and I was suddenly feeling lousy. My wife "left" me that night. I was bereft, lonely, sad, confused and feeling very stupid. I never saw it coming, this emotional mess I had got myself into. I was at a loss which I didn't expect and feeling very upset.

We actually had arranged this separation for some time and knew it was coming but neither of us expected to get into an emotionally distressed state about it, certainly not me. Of course, we had rarely been apart in thirty five years of marriage and so this was a relatively new experience for us. I had been in Pizzo for two weeks on my own in June but that did not affect me to the same degree in any way. There were reasons for that, I suppose

I had been waiting for months to come back to Pizzo, having

started buying the house last October. My June flight had been booked in January. I was coming over to complete the purchase of the house, the work on which had originally been scheduled to be completed by 1 June. Then, as it became clear that the work would not be finished on time the plan was that I would be here to put the pressure on, to have it completed as soon as possible. I was excited to be finally coming and starting my holiday also, a new kind of holiday for us, with our own foreign home. I was entranced when I arrived and kept myself busy checking the work and completing the purchase. The novelty kept me going maybe and meeting new people in a new situation. Then my wife joined me and we got used to being together Pizzo.

Now I was on my own again and missed her terribly. Pizzo did not do it for me any more without my wife! The sun was not shining that first morning after she left. She went on the night train to Rome to catch a flight early the next morning. Coming up to the day and time for her to go, we were feeling the coming separation but I did not expect to feel such powerful emotions. She had said she didn't want to go and dreaded the separation but I had just said we would manage and I fully expected to. I did not like the fact she was going on the night train but she had arranged it herself and was adamant it would be fine.

During the day I had arranged to get a lift for her to the station and we had a quiet enough day. She did her packing and preparations early and we went to the beach and relaxed afterwards as usual. There were serious problems at home with tenants of mine who were fighting and expected me to sort things out even though I was in Italy. I was getting texts and phone calls which had me worried and did not help but I was trying to keep it together. We went for a meal and she said her goodbyes to all our new friends in Pizzo before coming back to the house and waiting for our lift. When we went to the station we were there far too early and there was no ticket office but we just went for a drink with our kind driver and his friend. We drove back to the station in plenty of time and the tension of the oncoming separation became obvious. Like many men, I am not very good at handling the emotions and was probably afraid how it would go. Then I discovered the train was going to be late and started fretting about our friends who were waiting in the car to bring me back to Pizzo. Eventually, my wife just said to go and leave her wait for the train and she said goodbye to our waiting friends. It would make things easier to go now she said, and I agreed but still felt bad about it. Neither of us was in a great condition for tearful farewells and it made sense to cut it short but still I had misgivings for many reasons, guilt being one, of course. My friends suggested a late drink and I was in no condition to go to sleep so we did have a few. I texted her later and knew she got the train, which I had been worried about. She seemed to be fine.

I woke up early the next morning, sorrowful, worried and fretting about her and our other problems, but mainly simply feeling empty and lonely. I did not try to contact her as she might be sleeping or trying to get to the airport. She did text me to let me know she was at the airport and everything was ok. Unfortunately, it was not so with me. Worry, loneliness, distress and a level of depression set in and stayed with me for some time. I decided to go for a cappuccino to get out of the house but it did not work. I got upset at my usual breakfast bar and could not hold back the tears when someone enquired as to how I was feeling. He was very sympathetic and supportive before moving off, as was the girl in the bar whom we knew, when she saw my tears! I felt a right plonker but could not control it. That was my worst day in Pizzo this year, even worse than the disappointment of finding the work on the house not progressing, deadlines not being met, and promises not being kept

Later, I went back to the house and wrote my wife an email, expressing all my emotions. I just had to let it out, despite not wanting to worry her. An hour or two of vigorous housework helped and I went out for my usual swim. My wife phoned me to say she had arrived safely and to enquire as to how I was. She had known I was upset the previous night and she was worried about me. We consoled each other, saying we would learn from this and not go through it again. We won't go away in this way again I feel certain. We had discovered something about ourselves. The house in Pizzo will be great to have, but without each other it means little. My plans to come in October or at other times, even if my wife is not free, are now in shreds but I am glad to have learnt a certain reality, even if it was a harsh lesson. She phoned and emailed me back and it helped me to come to terms with my feelings. In one way it is a great testament to our relationship after 35 years of marriage. Is that what they call looking on the positive side?

In other circumstances it would have been the best of times. There had been genuine progress on the house at the time and a definite feeling it was going to be finished finally by the end of the week (only the fourth deadline!.. and the original one quoted to me when I first asked, after we signed the contract agreeing to buy it and do the reconstruction). We were both happy with it when we saw it on the day before Donna left, and even though Donna had not been able to get to live in it during her stay she was happy it would be ready when she came back with our first family group on 26 August.

August is the real tourist month when Pizzo is at its busiest and puts on a great show. On the day she left a photographic exhibition opened, a display of floral paintings was to be in the castle and a great street party was in preparation along a route close to our new house the following day. There would be food, drink and music provided along decorated and lit- up streets and Donna was disappointed to have to miss it all and many other events planned for the coming weeks. I was still around and could have been "having a ball". But I was not in the humour.

I did go to the party the following day as I just could not sit at home, crying into my beer. I decided to keep myself busy and to make an effort to get out of the black mood I was in and Donna had told me to enjoy Pizzo and all it had to offer because she was at home and it was grey, cold, wet and she was already bored! I first went to the photographic display and found it quite interesting. There were photos showing Pizzo Marina in winter with the waves crashing over the pier. Many beaches we had been to featured in the exhibition and there was a black and white section of photos, with personal portraits especially being absorbing. One photo of the town taken from a height was really impressive and an elaboration on it involving creative touches took my fancy also. It all kept me from dwelling on my personal problems for a while. The floral paintings in the castle were very colourful but did not grab my attention quite as well.

The street party was scheduled to start at 9pm and Sandro phoned me to come and meet him. He wanted to show me around. I did meet him and two of his friend and we started off but the start was delayed so we came back to the piazza. They were all speaking Italian and I felt out of it and so told them to go off themselves while I went on my own a little later. I actually went to the end of the route first but was given wine and food by some people I had got to know. There were musical groups at every station along the way and food and drink. A jazz group started off proceedings in the piazza and were very lively and I knew the songs and enjoyed them. A fortune teller who read cards was ensconced in a tunnel of drapes along the way and all the streets were decorated and colourfully lit. There were street performers on stilts to entertain the crowds as they made their way along. I eventually found where to buy the tickets for food and drink and paid just €5 for a bunch of tickets for everything. Pasta with n'Djua, punch bowl drinks, savouries and canapés, wine, slices of melon, sausages in panini, all accompanied by great humour and music made it a great night. I was sorry Donna was not with me to enjoy it and she would have loved it but I did manage to get into it and enjoy it myself.

In the days that followed I became very quiet and reserved. I kept to myself doing crosswords, sudoku, going for a swim everyday (but mostly not in the marina with the crowds), reading, writing, emailing and going on the internet, and checking on the progress on the house. It was a lonely time but there were some consolations. The house was finally getting finished and every day there were new developments. The furniture I had bought a few days ago arrived just as I was preparing to leave the house to give my first paying student of English her first lesson. She was home on holidays for two weeks and came to me every day for conversation mostly. I was glad to have something definite to do and to commence my teaching career in Italy. I had been advertising since I came in June and while some expressed interest nobody had followed through on it.

This student had come to me through Calabrian Invest, who were involved in property and had many plans for other services for English speaking customers and the general public in this area. They had started an internet café and an English monthly newsletter for which I wrote some articles and they had been very friendly and useful in many ways. Two of them, Paul and Lorraine, had driven us to the station for Donna to get the night train. There were four of them altogether and we had met and conversed many times and they were very encouraging about my teaching ambitions and had helped me to start an English language group who met in the Pantheon Bar every Monday night. The conversation group lasted for four weeks before petering out. It was mainly for my wife I had started it, as she felt in the need for conversation with fellow English speakers when she came first. I wanted it to be more of a language exchange group but it was proving difficult to attract sufficient Italians to it. In Dublin I had organised one in my local library and it was still going after eight years and sometimes I attended the ones in the ILAC centre library in central Dublin. They also kept me going when Donna was away in Ireland. They invited me to dinner on many occasions and proved to be real friends. Lorraine and Beata actually came to clean my house after it was finished and before Donna returned. Leon, the fourth member, sorted out another huge problem.

So the house was finally finished in August. My teaching career in Italy had begun, however humbly. The weather was still brilliant and it should have been a great time but my wife's departure had left me reeling. It is very strange when you finally get what you have wanted for a long time and then you get kicked by life and the hoped-for happiness proves illusory. Truly, "Life is what happens when you are making plans" (John Lennon). August was a difficult month but I felt at the time it would get better when my wife arrived back with our first family guests.

There was one more major item to be dealt with before I could relax completely, I felt. I had bought a kitchen along with other purchases in "Trony", a local outlet, in early June, but it had not been delivered. It was to be delivered the second week in August and did not arrive. Phone calls produced no response at all and worry set in that it would not be in place for the visit of my family on 26 August. Again my Italian friend, Sandro, came to the rescue. I asked him to bring me to the outlet and we went on Saturday, 16 August. The manager assured me he would phone me on the following Monday and he did. When I told him I had not been able to get an answer on the phone he said they had phone problems. Sandro did not believe that story but we were happy enough with the assurances.

The phone call on the Monday had cheered me up a lot but, unfortunately, the kitchen delivery did not occur. On Tuesday I received a phone call to say it was on its way. A van arrived into the piazza about an hour later. It parked there and some guys came to see where exactly the house was. They told a friend, Francesco, who was with me, that they would have to go back and get a smaller van to deliver the stuff nearer my house because the van was too big for the small alleys of the centro storico. I believed they would just change around and be back in an hour or two. They did not come back that day. About 3 hours later, I got young Carmen who worked for the summer in the Pantheon Bar to ring for me. It was the delivery company phone number I had, as Trony, where I had bought it, were not answering phone calls just like last week. The delivery company man said he would have to talk to Trony and would deliver my kitchen and other purchases that day or the next.

I was far from happy with that but had not the requisite Italian to let him know or argue the point. Nothing is easy about doing business here at times, especially without the language. One has to learn to go with the flow and not let it get one down when it doesn't happen but to enjoy the positives of Italian life, like sun, sea, beaches, food, and the laid-back lifestyle, especially in Calabria. When the kitchen was not delivered that day I found it hard to do just that.

Well, the kitchen did not arrive and phone calls proved useless; in fact, were not even answered. Eventually, my friend Sandro, came to my rescue again and drove me to Trony again (for the fifth time). I had a good "go" at the boss in my limited Italian and he just took it calmly. Finally, Sandro suggested we arrange transportation ourselves, through another friend of his. The store boss was very glad to accept this and promised to provide a worker to instal the kitchen. We arranged for the transportation successfully and it arrived on Friday, 22 August, but, of course, the worker did not turn up, despite more promises. I called Leon, one of the four in Calabrian Invest and asked him to help. He installed the kitchen over three days. We were still at it half an hour before my wife and some family members arrived on Monday 25 August.

Yes, they arrived a day earlier than I expected which led to some panic as the kitchen was not yet fully finished. My wife had planned to arrive in Rome on Monday 25 August and to get the night train so as to arrive the next day. That plan was changed and she got the train at midday and arrived with my son and daughter and her boyfriend at about 7 pm on the Monday. It was a very busy day for us all. A bed arrived, the final part of my purchases from Trony, courtesy of Sandro's friend, Graziano. Earlier Leon and Beata had gone to Vibo to buy some more supplies needed to instal the kitchen. The worktop arrived separately about 5 pm, when we were still finishing off the kitchen installation. Leon had to cut out the sink and hob sections and the blades were not lasting well. Beata was cleaning again. All the time I was getting texts about the train journey and arrival. Panic may have set in at some stage but at about 6.30pm Beata had to stop her cleaning to collect the arrivals from the station. I couldn't go as there would not have been room in the car coming back and I was still trying to get the kitchen finished with Leon. A mini-disaster struck as the work top broke when we lifted it to put it in place! A quick decision was made to leave it to another day and I went to welcome my wife and family to Pizzo. What a day!

CHAPTER 10
August : The Family Arrive

The excitement was great when Donna, my wife, came to our new house in Pizzo, along with Anna, my daughter and her boyfriend Liam, and my son Mark. They were thrilled with the house and it was great to have it all finished for them. They found it roomy and bright and were soon forgetting their tiredness after their long plane journey from Dublin to Naples and the train down to Pizzo. It was the end of August so there were still many holidaymakers around and festivities had not completely ceased. That night we just wandered down to the piazza and had a meal and some drinks. They told me about their journey and also remarked on how calm and unstressed I was and that I had lost a lot of weight, which I had not realised.

It was great to introduce them to all my new friends in Pizzo as well as the delights of the beaches, the bars, the ice cream and the laid- back lifestyle. My wife had been worried about us providing enough activities and excitement for them but, after the wet summer in Ireland they had been through, the simple pleasures of sun, sand, swimming, sun-bathing and cheap food and drink completely enthralled them and they were very contented.

Every day they went to the beach for a swim, sometimes twice. They ate out mostly but Sandro came once to show them how to make great carbonara in our new kitchen. We hired a car for a week and went out to Marinella to the lovely restaurant on the beach Sandro had brought Donna and me to. The friends we had made in Pizzo made them very welcome and sometimes they went out with them themselves and also stayed out longer than us at night. On another day we brought them to Tropea where we had been on holiday the previous year. The sun shone, the waves rolled in and the sand was sparking clean. We also wandered around the old town and it was a marvellous day. On the night before Mark went back, we went to a more expensive restaurant just outside Pizzo. We got a great selection of starters and sat out, looking out to sea from a high veranda. Lights shone brilliantly on the sea and life seemed too good to be true. “Why couldn’t it always be like this?”, we mused.

The sleeping and living arrangements worked out well; Mark sleeping in the room behind the terraza, on the second floor; Donna and I in our bedroom at the back of the first floor, and Anna and Liam in the front one, leaving downstairs to anybody who wished to stay up late or get up earlier than others. Also we had the communal entrance and exit between us and the people next door, so we could come and go without disturbing each other. Showers and toilets were on two floors and the kitchen and sitting room on the ground floor were available to us all. There was also a small cooking area and sink on the first floor.

Bernard, my second son, and Olive his partner, came along for our last ten days in Pizzo in 2008. They brought their 6 month old baby, Anna Marie, with them. Anna and Liam had a day or two with them before returning home. We had the car which helped a bit but we did not undertake any long journeys with such a young baby. Mostly we stayed in during the heat of the midday sun and went for a swim at four or five o’clock. Even Anna Marie got into the water and loved it. It had been a worry that the baby would find the heat and the whole adventure too much but she was great and revelled in it. We, as grandparents, helped out with babysitting, of course, but it was great to have us all together. Bernard displayed his culinary skills and we appreciated the food he cooked in our own kitchen. I vowed to learn Italian cooking.

We had our friends from Calabrian Invest, Paul, Lorraine, Leon and Beata, to our house for dinner and drinks on the last night. It was a great night and I think they really enjoyed it. We served them roast beef as it was a long time since they had had a really British dish. They told us to keep in contact and promised to look after our house when we were gone. We gave them the keys. Beata’s family were coming to stay in our house for a week the next day. Sandro and Siena, our good friends, came to bring us to the station the next day for our return to Ireland. We got the train to Rome and on out to the airport. It was a long day and had been an especially long holiday for me. But now we had purchased and lived in our Italian house and were going home to Ireland. “Veni, Vidi, Vici”, a dream had been realised!

Three generations of Powers outside SPQR and La Ruota ...
and Olive of course!

Calabrian Invest: Paul, Beata, Lorraine and Leon; great friends and a great help to to us in so many ways, not least feeding me when Donna was not there

Myself on the beach

Seggiola bay ... a favourite seaside seat of Cicero's ... and yours truly

Looking out from the sun terrace over the roofs and out to sea

Leon and his mate stride across the piazza
after a hard day working on a thirst

Bernard, Anna Marie and Granny in the sea at dusk

Romance in a golden sunset sea … guess who's minding the baby?

Another happy couple.
Bernard, Olive and Anna Marie out after dark

The happy couple in the swim on their honeymoon

Bernard, son number 2 and his daughter
Anna Marie ... only a few months

Mark on his favourite rock in the sea … chilling!

Franco and Carmen of the Pantheon
("International" as he says). Great friends

Myself, my son Mark and Liam, who married Anna ...
bonding over drinks

The crowded beach in August

Donna and Anna, who enjoyed her honeymoon in Pizzo …
after we arrived!

The new front door of house

The inner metal stair with tufo-stone base
on the ground floor sitting room

The tiles are laid on the second floor ...
great but when will it all be done?

The architect and building manager, Mr Plant, and I
when it is all over

The Pantheon Bar, great for birra alla spina ...
and on to the main shopping corso

Crowds for the blessing of the boats
on a beautiful Sunday in Pizzo harbour

Our friends Sara and Salvatore watching the match in the piazza ... great nights!

The newly plastered and painted wall, a beautiful sight for me after a long wait

A view from the piazza to the harbour and beach below where we swim

Donna at the beach enjoying the sun … protecting the face with a hat

Donna arrives in Pizzo, outside our temporary apartment in June 2008

Sunset on sea and boats ... a cool time of day for just being out and about

Scaffolding on the front wall, old front door and window gone! Progress at last!

Religious procession makes its way around the town ... it is Festa time!

Franco, who was first to call me a “Pizzitano”
and his father in Bar Ercole

One of our Bulgarian workers working on side wall.
New roof looks well

CHAPTER 11
Back in Dublin

We came back to Dublin in September 2009. Back in Dublin, sunny Pizzo seems so far away already. The weather, all dark skies and rain, is depressing. Days become shorter and dim evenings start earlier. Winter approaches. Jobs are being lost and salaries cut. The value of pension funds is slashed. House prices are collapsing. The world economic system is in freefall. Lives are being ruined and reality is biting hard.

At night we sit in watching tv and worrying about our savings and living costs. The price of food and ordinary shopping is astronomical compared to Pizzo. We almost give up eating out after paying €90 for a very average meal which we would have got in Pizzo for less than €20. A plate of pasta which I got for €5 or less costs anything between €10 and €25 in Dublin.

Tidying up and sorting the house keeps me occupied for a while. There is a new M50 toll pass to be paid. I find it hard to try explaining myself and my holiday to people. They tell me I am looking well but I feel brutal. I am conflicted and a bit lost. I am not even interested in drinking as I have lost weight and want to keep it that way. Thinking of the future in this climate is not a good idea. Are my investments safe as banks tumble about? The guarantee to the banks by the Irish government is not very reassuring really. Do I have enough money for retirement?

It was cheaper to live in Italy and retirement there could be an option but would it be a matter of feeling lost in two countries? I would miss my grandchildren and children if I stayed in Italy. My children are dealing with serious life problems here due to the economic downturn, babies, child care, housing. Mortgages are harder to get even if prices are cheaper. I do have responsibilities here too. Who would look after my house here? Staying here is depressing, however, and I do worry about the house in Italy too.

I wanted a simpler life but buying the house has made it more complicated, it seems. For the past year it took up a lot of my free time and energy. Now I need new interests and activities. My wife and I are at a new stage of life and have more time for ourselves but I am bored here and finding daily life a sad grind. Depression is all around. The contrast between our lives in Pizzo and here is immense. I know it was a holiday but I am retired now and could be there full time if I wanted. Decisions have to be made and I am finding it difficult. Not being with my wife was the worst part and she still works here in Ireland. But I am not getting any younger and should I just take this opportunity to enjoy the latter years of my life?

I know I need to improve my Italian in order to really communicate and live there properly if I want to be able to socialise and do business. It is not so easy but the possibilities are there. There are still matters to be dealt with as regards the house in Pizzo, such as local taxes and electricity bills, and although minor they are still worries. It is very hard to deal with them from here.

The whole process of viewing, buying and reconstructing the house took up a very busy year in my life but I am delighted with the house. Life goes on here in Dublin and I dream about Pizzo still. We will go back next year and intend to have some time there on our own, just my wife and I. In all the time there this year we never had that and it will be the real test for us. Family and friends can come at other times and I think we may start renting it to people through our friends in Calabrian Invest. The adventure goes on. It has left me exhilarated at times and also brought me to the edge of depression. Now that the house is bought and completed the future should be simpler but who can tell?

Anyway, we have followed our dream. We have tried the T shirt, bought the house and I wouldn't change it now for the world but it was a lot more difficult than I thought it would be.

EPILOGUE

May, 2009

"The world is too much with us; late and soon,
Getting and spending, we lay waste our powers:
Little we see in Nature that is ours;
We have given our hearts away, a sordid boon!
This sea that bares her bosom to the moon;
The winds that will be howling at all hours,
And are up-gathered now like sleeping flowers;
For this, for everything, we are out of tune,
It moves us not.--**Great God! I'd rather be**
A Pagan suckled in a creed outworn;
So might I, standing on this pleasant lea,
Have glimpses that would make me less forlorn;
Have sight of Proteus rising from the sea;
Or hear old Triton blow his wreathed horn.

William Wordsworth

I am writing this chapter a year later, after our first week back in Pizzo since we bought the house in 2008. My sister has accompanied us this time and is exhilarated by the place "All this and heaven too!" as she says herself. The sun has shone all week and we have been on the beach and swam in the clear, blue water which is certainly cooler than I remember it from June to September last year, but oh! it is so refreshing. The locals do not seem to care for it when it is cold and we have had the beach to ourselves almost, apart from a few other tourists. We are cooking more for ourselves and adding to our kitchen facilities and equipment. My sister made pesto from basil, mayonnaise, garlic and pine nuts on the advice of a local restaurateur and it was lovely to have it so fresh and tasty, much superior to the bottle version. Normally we make our own lunch and go out to eat in the evening and have pasta. The piazza is quiet mostly as it is not the tourist season yet. We are staying for three weeks and will be joined by Mark and his girlfriend for the last week. We will return again in

August and stay until the middle of September.

Our daughter Anna is getting married to Liam in July in Ireland so we must be home for that and preparations have been in full swing since last year. They will come here for the honeymoon at the end of July and we will join them a few days later. My other daughter who has been in Australia for about 18 months is coming home in July for the wedding. Her boyfriend, Dom, will be with her so it will be an exciting time. They will also come to Pizzo for a week before returning to Australia. We still have to decide whether to let it when we are not using it. Our Calabrian Express friends could do that for us but I think it will be let only to our friends and theirs.

Little has changed in Pizzo apart from a few shops and a new parking meter system. Work on the lift from the marina to the piazza is proceeding which would be a great advantage to us all, as climbing up and down steps can be tiring. My wife is most excited about that. It was promised in election material last year and it seems not all election promises are useless (or so we hoped). Our Italian friends are delighted to see us and also our friends in Calabrian Invest, who had the care of our house and keys. They sorted our electricity for us which had been disconnected because of our failure to pay the bill, due to not having received the first one when we were last in Pizzo. The first bill must be paid personally in the post office and then can be paid through a bank order or whatever. So there is much to be learned about living in Italy and particularly maybe about buying a house in this area. I hope the following advice is useful to some of you.

- Learn Italian. The amount of people I see who have no Italian and expect to live here is amazing. I find it hard to believe they expect to socialise, integrate or even just manage and/or enjoy life here.
- Originally, I always said I would rent first and try out a place before buying. I didn't exactly do that but I did come here many times before buying and I had stayed in an apartment in

Tropea for 3 weeks and also in a B/B here. So I strongly suggest prospective buyers should live in the place they think they might buy in, before committing to it.

- It is easier to make friends and integrate in a small community so big cities might be more difficult to settle in if you want to really go Italian. Some people don't really want or need that, just the sun, beach, Italian food etc but for me it was important to be in among the locals and not in a tourist village or in a situation with lots of "ex-pats".
- Tourist villages such as we have here in Pizzo are generally a few kilometres outside the centro storico. They have good facilities such as pools, tennis courts etc but while I would enjoy that, my priority was to be near the main piazza with all its life and near the beach, but among the local Italians. Others may have different priorities. The tourist villages are mostly empty outside the season and can be lonely, desolate places at times. Even in summer, but especially in winter, ex-pats can spend their time drinking, bemoaning Italy and its perceived deficiencies and Italians, and keeping to themselves, mainly because they couldn't be bothered to learn the language or were not open to the charms of the real Italy. We tried one in Pescara in September one year and were put off by what we found.
- The process of buying a house or apartment is different for everybody. Many people come to Italy with estate agents on a free trip and are only shown new properties developed by that company. We have seen such people and they are often stressed out, not allowed to leave the company of those agents, followed around and kept in check, and are pressured into buying off plans often and at a price much in excess of what they could get by going to the trouble of finding properties themselves or with the help of local Italian agents. Even then the properties are often not built on time and it is difficult, if not impossible, to get deposits refunded if they are not satisfied or there are problems. We viewed many properties on various holidays in Italy. Local agents were very kind and

drove us around whenever we wished to view their properties. Talking to them we learned a lot and it helped us to crystallise what we wanted, a rustico or new build, in the centro storico or at the beach, an apartment or house etc. Viewing and discussing all costs nothing and can be interesting for many reasons, on holiday. I suggest it is better than coming on a viewing weekend, paid for by the company maybe, but with their agenda in mind, not yours.

- I would strongly suggest getting a local agent, maybe through the internet, but one with English (or your native language) and Italian connections so you can discuss matters in your own language. Even doing that we had some problems but without the language it is very difficult to operate in Italy. Our agent set up a bank account for us, a "codice fiscale" which is needed to do any business in Italy, translated for us and made travel and other arrangements for us. Her husband checked out the title of the property and the work done, as he was a geometra (type of architect used in Italy in property conveyancing). He also advised us in many ways, as did his wife, and smoothed the dealings with the supervisor of works, telling us when to relent and when to "stick to our guns".
- Notaio: the official who completes the deed of purchase and who must be satisfied everything is in order and who tries to protect the purchaser also if not both parties. He or she must be paid, of course, and the bill will be several thousands of euro. It is useful to have a local person do this so you don't have to travel too far. Your agent might consider this when you talk to him/her.
- A deposit is usually paid to reserve the property. It may have conditions so beware. As a purchaser you can also include your conditions. We got our Irish solicitor, who had some Italian, to check it and the contract also. We made it a condition of sale and return of our deposit, that we would get our sun terrace. Unfortunately, we did not include a date for completion of work in our contract and it might have helped. I don't know if it would have been acceptable anyway to our

builder but it could have been tried.

- Contract: Our contract was signed within a month or two of us agreeing to buy. It is one of the stages of purchasing the house and it is important to check it out thoroughly, both the original and the translation. Mistakes will happen, as with us, even with an agent who had English, but careful reading and asking questions can sort out a lot. Specify wooden or metal stairs for example, or price of tiles and fittings, boilers and radiators or air conditioning, which can also provide heat. Fitted kitchens are not usually supplied with houses and showers may not include doors etc. Italians like heavy front doors for security and have their own ideas on houses and apartments which we may not share. Look into everything, if possible, and even chat to other prospective buyers. If you are opting for a new build in a tourist estate/villagio it may not be possible to make changes, but they usually come set up for non-Italians and aimed at a specific market, eg British or French or German, and are more likely to include kitchen facitities.
- Works payments. There are staged payments which must be met. Cash payments are allowed as well as cheques and this may help reduce bills.
- It would be wise to retain or delay some final payments until all work is checked and a "snag" list drawn up and worked through, just as at home.
- Bank cards: they are useful when you have an Italian bank account for withdrawing money and paying bills. Ours had a daily limit of €250 and a monthly limit of €1500. When setting up house these can be easily increased as the need arises.
- Internet banking is available and could prove very useful as are direct debits and /or standing orders for payment of bills like gas and electricity. Gas and electricity must be connected and ordered in advance. Water, postal facilities and local taxes must be arranged for. Gas connection is slow I am advised but bottle gas can be used temporarily or even permanently, thus saving connections and standing charges. However, gas is cheaper than electricity according to my Italian friends.

- It is important to greet and meet Italians, especially neighbours, who can be very useful in minding your property when you are away and watering plants etc. It depends on your attitude and agenda, I suppose, but for me it was what I wanted and I found them to be very hospitable and friendly. I may have gone further than most people, having a t-shirt made with "Sono Pizzitano" (I am a man of Pizzo) emblazoned on it. I got known very quickly then, and also because I went down to the piazza to watch football and drink with all the locals during the European Championships of 2008 when Spain won. So when my wife joined me we had many ready-made friends. Most were very glad to welcome and help us and even went out of their way to do so.
- Another way to get involved is to join classes or groups, even of foreign groups of students or adult learners. Having a sport like tennis to play also made a difference for us. Sailing, singing, karaoke, dancing, fishing, a ceramics course or any activity that gets you involved can only increase your chances of making it all work out for you in a foreign land.
- Italian food and cooking is famous world-wide so it would be a pity to ignore it. Fruit and vegetables come fresh and in season and are very good value. Markets occur every week and are great meeting places and social occasions of getting to know people. In Pizzo we go every Thursday and buy a lot of stuff for the house and for the week ahead. There is a bigger one in Vibo on a Saturday and a lovely pedestrian street in which to shop or relax afterwards. My wife shops and I indulge my ice cream and/or beer appetite.
- Meat is available in the supermarkets but also from small butcher shops which can provide you with good, safe, local produce. They have not disappeared as much in Italy as in Ireland or England.
- Fish is in great supply at seaside towns and is usually very fresh and relatively cheap. In Pizzo we go at 18.30 to our local fish merchant and get prawns, mussels, clams, swordfish, tuna and many other varieties in season, depending on the weather.

- Bus and train travel is cheap and mostly dependable, except maybe in the tourist season though more buses are usually put in service then, even free ones. Local buses often bring one to market or nearby towns. It is good to purchase tickets before getting on the bus, at tabacchi shops or kiosks. The trains go all over and a Trenitalia website gives information but sometimes it is fails to work, not recognising certain stations because of use of improper names or not allowing payment with foreign credit cards. I have found it useful but also frustrating. Certain places are easier to get to by train, such as Vernazza in Le Cinque Terre. There are even free buses organised for the summer season which can be used to get to the beach or to other tourist or local spots
- In northern Italy punctuality and order may be as we expect it to be in major cities in Germany, Holland and even England and Ireland at times, but in Southern Italy and in Pizzo I have found it to be less important and this could be infuriating if you let it get to you. A laid-back lifestyle and a lack of urgency is a characteristic of a lot of Calabrese, even architects, builders, other professionals, bus drivers and so on. One can complain and criticise but I found it got me nowhere and it is better to become more relaxed oneself. "If you can't beat them, join them" might be a good motto. Trying to convert the locals to our standards might be a huge mistake and anyway we come here because we enjoy the calmer pace of life so why change it? Believe me, it is not my usual modus operandi but I have learned to go with the flow, well… mostly.
- The catholic religion still has a great hold on the people but it is more a community activity and sense of inherited culture and all sorts join the community in regular processions and celebrations, usually culminating in a ceremony or mass in the piazza, before, during and after which eating and drinking continue all around. Fireworks often finish proceedings (and this may explain loud booms one hears on the mornings of feast days and weddings as they practise etc.). They hold onto their customs and beliefs and are better for it, I believe,

although the young are not flocking to mass or anything like that and it could all disappear soon. That would be a pity, and I say that though I am not a religious person.

- Local taxes are not so expensive and are based on the rateable valuation of the property when sold. So in the centro storico they may be less as old buildings retain their old valuation and that may be very little. However they must be paid at the post office, twice yearly and by both partners if bought in both their names.
- Calabria is being discovered much more now and the price of property, food and ordinary living is generally less than in other areas. Many English and Irish are settling in the area. In Spain it happened years ago but we hope much has been learned from the experience. Who wants it to turn into an arena for cheap boozing, big apartment blocks, the excesses of youth culture and worse? So please resist the urge to change it too much and let us hope the Italian authorities realise what they have and do not opt for the cheap money and easy way out. Strict building regulations exist and should be maintained especially in the centro storico.
- Respect the culture you have come to and its citizens if you wish to live here (and learn the language!). We don't really need the all-day British or Irish breakfast, the Premiership, Irish pubs (unless they are staffed by real Irish), and so on. Italian style and design, food and drink, song, music and dance, history and architecture, sport, and above all language are what we want and expect when we come on holiday or to live here.
- Finally, may I wish you all the best of luck in your Italian adventures, whether you buy property or not. I do not believe it is for everybody but people must discover this for themselves. Renting is a good option, especially over a long period and if pursued with a view to eventually buying. Italy has so much to offer despite the state of the economy and its other problems. Viva Italia!

Glossary

A la passegiata: as for a walk.. the evening stroll beloved by Italians ..a dressy one

Alici: sardines, small fish often marinated and served as a starter

"Amo (ti) Pizzo": I love (you) Pizzo

Angola cottura: a small cooking corner or area, with sink, cooker or hob, etc.

Acqua frizzante: sparkling water

"Basta": "enough". .used to correct children ..and to tell that you are finished eg when shopping for many items or ordering

Bilocale: an apartment with 2 bedrooms

Birra grande: large beer , but often one gets a medium sized beer (eg 400 cl) instead (birra medea) as a real birra grande is so big (about a litre or 2 pints)

Birra medea: see above

Birra piccolo: small beer, about 200 cl.

Camorra: a gang like the mafia, based in Naples probably

Cavaliero: a gentleman..a knight

Centro storico: historic centre

Certamente: certainly

Cippola: onion.. the red onions of Tropea are particularly famous

Civile Protezione: civil guards or local wardens

Commune: council of a town like Pizzo

Cornetto: brioche, croissant, a breakfast pastry

Corso: a main street.. a shopping street in Pizzo..

Diario: diary

Dolci: confectionary or sweet things such as cakes. desserts etc

Domani: tomorrow.. a favourite word.. used as a concept of time such as "manana" .. tomorrow or ... sometimes or never?

Fagioli:	beans ..either broad beans or "fagiolini" which are runner beans
Festa Fragole:	strawberry festival
Gelateria:	ice cream vendor / parlour / bar
Gentile:	kind or good ..as in gentleman maybe
Immobiliare:	usually refers to an estate agency
Le Cinque Terre:	5 villages on the Ligurian Sea, above La Spezia. They are famous for the cultivation of vegetables in a special tiered way and a world heritage site, I believe. Vernazza is one where we stayed.
Mezzogiorno:	literally mid-day but often refers to a state of mind, especially as used when referring to the south of Italy, ie a; lazy, sleepy time, with nothing much happening
Monolocale:	a one bedroom apartment
Mozzarella:	a cheese for which Italy is famous..white and it comes in various sizes and dishes
n'Djou:	a piquant sauce or meat .. a speciality of Pizzo and Calabria
Notaio:	a notary public, or official who checks a contract of sale and stamps it to make it official
Omerta:	a vow or practice of silence in relation to mafia-type activities
Palazzo:	a palace or fine big house
Pescatore:	fisherman
Piano:	a floor or storey of a building
"Piano piano":	slowly, slowly; or bit by bit
Poco italiano:	a little Italian .. a little grasp of the language
Polpetta di carne:	a pulped meat snack
Prosciutto crudo:	ham.. a type of ..as in parma ham.. raw, crude or "uncured": there is also a prosciutto cotto which is cooked or cured ham, as we know of in Ireland
Prosecco:	a sparkling white wine

Risotto alla Pescatore:	Rice dish with seafood eg mussels and clams (cozze e vongole), often requires 2 diners at least to order it in a restaurant
Rustico:	an old or rustic building, a term used to describe one which could be renovated and/or rebuilt to form a house or apartment
"Sono insegnante Inglese, di Irlanda":	I am a teacher of English from Ireland
Tabacchi:	a tobacconist's shop ..but in Italy it is also the place to buy bus tickets and lots more
Turistico Villagio:	tourist village, usually with many facilities such as swimming pools, tennis courts, restaurants etc and usually populated by foreigners often based on nationality eg French, German, English. They are often situated a few kilometres outside the town.
Salsiccia piccante:	a piquant sausage or salami
"Sono Pizzitano":	I am a man of Pizzo
Vecchio/a:	old person: man or woman